DARING
ADVENTURES

A New Creation Story
for Trans and Non-Binary People

based on a poem by The Rev. Asher O'Callahan

In the beginning, God created day and night.
But have you ever seen a sunset?
Trans and non-binary people are kind of like sunsets.
Full of a hundred shades of color you can't see
in plain daylight or during the dark night.

In the beginning, God created land and sea.
But have you ever seen a beach?
Trans and non-binary people are kind of like beaches,
an oasis that's not quite like the ocean,
nor quite like the land.

In the beginning, God created birds of the
air and fish of the sea.
But have you ever seen a flying fish,

or a seagull,
or a puffin that swims and flies?
Trans and non-binary people are kind of like
those amazing creatures.
We spend our time between the water and the land,
creative combinations of characteristics
that blows people's minds.

In the beginning God created male and female,
in God's own image, God created them.
So in the same way God created people
with genders beyond male and female,
in God's own image, God created them.

God created people
cis, trans, non-binary, a-gender and intersex,
in between, outside of, and beyond
night and day, land and sea, fish and bird.

All different sorts of people, all different
sorts of relationships,
God created them from love, to love, and to be loved.
God created them all in God's own image,
And God is still creating them.

DARING ADVENTURES

Helping Gender-Diverse Kids and Their Families Thrive

RACHEL A. CORNWELL

Daring Adventures
Helping Gender-Diverse Kids and Their Families Thrive

by Rachel A. Cornwell

Edited by Gregory F. Augustine Pierce
Designed and typeset by Andrea Reider
Front cover designed by Wendy Hudgins, wendyhudgins.com
Front cover artwork "Image" by Geordanna Cordero on Unsplash
Family photo by Elisse Lassiter, elisse@myglimmerimages.com

Some of the names and situations in this book have been changed to
protect the privacy of non-public people, and conversations with the
author are to the best of her recollection and attested as to the truth
of their content.

Published by ACTA Publications, www.actapublications.com,
800-397-2282.

Library of Congress Catalog number: 1022951884
ISBN: 978-0-87946-699-2
Printed in the United States of America by Total Printing Systems
Year 30 29 28 27 26 25 24 23
Printing 10 9 8 7 6 5 4 3 2 First
Text printed on 30% post-consumer recycled paper

CONTENTS

Introduction   1

The Lucky Ones   13

Choices   25

Go with the Flow   37

The Whole Family Transitions   55

Schools, Sex Ed, Sleepovers, and More   67

A Spectrum of Gender-Affirming Care   87

Dating and Sexuality   103

Speaking up/Speaking Out   113

Afterword   125

Some Helpful Terms   127

Recommendations for Further Reading   131

Suggestions for Faith Communities   133

Acknowledgments   137

About the Author   139

For all the gender-diverse kids.
May you always know how loved you are.

For Nora, Graham, and Evan.
I am so lucky to be your mom.

INTRODUCTION

Life is either a daring adventure or nothing.

Helen Keller

She was the friend of a neighbor, someone I'd never even met, and yet she was pouring her heart out to me over the phone. Her thirteen-year-old had—seemingly out of the blue—told his parents that he was not a girl, but a boy. The child had already chosen a new name and different pronouns. The mother, a deeply faithful woman, told me, "It's not possible for my child to be transgender. We're Christians."

Part of this parent's struggle to accept her child's gender exploration came from her perception that transgender issues and people are suddenly everywhere; that this change in her child was caused by some cultural trend. She thought her religious values should have shielded her child from varying from the traditional norms around gender and sexuality, but they had not. Her son was figuring out who he was and how he would express himself, whether or not that conformed to his parent's expectations and beliefs.

⁓

Although it's not always been as visible as it is now, transgender and gender-non-conforming people have been part of every culture and every community since, well, forever. In the past few years, gender diversity is starting to be more accepted in the world (albeit also more controversial in some circles), and transgender and non-binary young people are now much more visible in popular culture. They now have the space, the terminology, and the role models to help them live openly as their authentic selves. While transgender and non-binary people statistically make up less than 1% of the population of the United States, the highest percentage of individuals identifying as transgender and non-binary are currently between the ages of thirteen and seventeen.[1] Transgender and non-binary persons belong to every racial ethnic group, every class and geographic region, and (this surprises many people) every religion and political persuasion. They are our neighbors and co-workers, friends, family members, and yes, our children.

But religious and cultural influences can still make it more difficult for young people to "come out," to recognize

---

[1] "Age of Individuals Who Identify as Transgender in the United States" The Williams Institute, UCLA School of Law, 2017

and affirm their gender identity. Being a Christian, for example, doesn't mean you can't, or aren't, or won't be transgender. But it can mean that your family and/or your community may not as readily accept who you are. Being a Christian, especially if your experience of Christianity is more socially and theologically conservative, in fact, can lead to greater instances of rejection by parents, families, and faith communities who cannot reconcile their religious beliefs with a child's evolving gender identity.

This rejection of gender diversity extends beyond family and interpersonal relationships, too, as religiously-based bigotry against transgender people has been enacted into law. In 2022, there were more than 300 bills introduced in thirty-five states across the nation that targeted transgender children, youth and their families. These laws are largely backed by social conservatives, many of whom are evangelical and mainline Christians. The first laws in the country banning transgender girls and women from participating on female sports teams and preventing parents and medical professionals from treating transgender minors with gender-affirming medical care were passed in 2021 in my home state of Arkansas, a bastion of conservative Christianity. Yet at the same time, I have friends and colleagues from all over the country contacting me with increasing frequency or seeking support for a another parent who is struggling with their child's gender questioning or transition.

I am writing this book for those kids exploring their gender identity, especially the ones who live in communities that are not as open and affirming of gender diversity, and for those families with gender-diverse kids looking for support, guidance, and hope that they and their kids are going to be OK. If you are reading this book, it's likely that you share my commitment to learning, growing, and creating more safe spaces where these kids and families will be welcomed with open arms and surrounded with the love and support they need and deserve.

As the parent of a transgender child (as well as two other children who are cisgender, which means they identify as the gender that was assigned to them at birth) and as a Christian pastor, I take it as part of my calling to help parents and families of gender-diverse kids hold on to their faith while also fully accepting and affirming their children. As the American culture in general has become more accepting of the spectrum of gender identity, we still see that faith communities of all denominations and traditions not only lag behind in understanding and acceptance but also often cause great damage to their own followers because of misinformation, poor theological reflection, and lack of openness to the creative mystery of the human experience. We harm our children, we cause brokenness in our families, and we diminish our public witness and relationship with a God of love and acceptance. While only .7% of youth between the age of thirteen and seventeen in the U.S. identify as transgender, one-third to one-half of those same kids will at one point in their beautiful lives consider suicide, partly because they experience rejection from their families, religious institutions, and communities.[2]

It doesn't have to be this way.

If you are a parent who is also a person of faith and your child is exploring his/her/their gender identity, I want to offer you this word of hope: You don't have to choose between your child and your faith. You do not have to reject your child because your faith tradition has taught you that being non-conforming in one's gender identity is not natural or part of "God's design." You do not have to give up your faith just because you love and affirm and want to protect your child. Being a believer and loving and fully accepting your child are compatible. Trust me on this.

⁓

But. You will have to learn new things. Your faith may need to be stretched and changed. You might need to find a different faith community to participate in. You will have to give up your own preconceived notions about your child and your role as his/her/their parent.

And. It will be worth it. I speak from experience when I tell you that your children will all thrive, no matter what

---

[2] "National Survey on LGBTQ Youth Mental Health," The Trevor Project, 2020

their gender identity. They will love themselves and be happier, healthier, and more resilient if you are able to accept them for who they are. I promise you will find a community of parents, advocates, and transgender and non-binary people who will teach you much and expand your view of the world and of the varieties of human experience. Your faith will deepen and grow as you come to see that God's creation is even more diverse and wondrous than any of us ever thought it could be.

⌒

So, before you read any further, I'd like to share a little more about myself and also offer some definitions of terms that I'll be using throughout this book.

As I said previously, I am a mother and a Christian pastor. I grew up in, was ordained, and serve in the United Methodist Church. Methodists are a mainline Christian denomination who are currently engaged in a schism over human sexuality and may, in the next year or so, divide over this issue.

The specific congregation I grew up in during the 1980s and early 1990s was in the South, and while it was not particularly conservative—socially or theologically— it was not (at least at the time) an LGBTQ+ affirming church. I don't remember ever hearing a sermon on homosexuality or transgender identity. Mine was the kind of church that would say "all are welcome" but, given the time, the social and geographic location, and the average age of the congregation, it was a place where traditional Christian values were taught and reinforced, both overtly and subtly. My fellow congregants were, and continue to be good, loving people. They taught me to love God and my neighbor, to be forgiving and honest, to ask questions and seek deeper wisdom. I am grateful for the spiritual foundation I received in this church.

I went to a United Methodist affiliated college, also in the South, and after serving as a young-adult mission volunteer in Japan and Washington, DC, I went to a United Methodist seminary in Atlanta, Georgia. My formation as a Christian and as a pastor, therefore, has been pretty traditional and middle-of-the-road. I am also white, upper-middle class, highly educated, happily heterosexual, and blessed with a traditional Christian marriage. (I share all this to assure you that I am not some radical activist with an agenda. I am, perhaps, a lot like you.)

My husband, Marcus, and I had two children, a girl, Nora, and then a boy, Graham. Both healthy, delightful children. But we felt that our family was not yet complete. So we added a third, a child we thought for five years was a girl; but, as it turns out, Evan is very much a boy.

Evan was, even as a baby, our most daring child. He was the only child who required us to baby-proof our house. He started swimming before he could walk and rode a bike without training wheels at the age of three. His favorite phrase as a toddler was "I do it." He is brave and bold and headstrong. As a preschooler, he rejected anything that was typically, in his words, "girly": clothes, toys, activities. For Halloween when he was three, he insisted on being Superman, and corrected anyone who asked if he was dressed up as Supergirl. ("NO! I Super-MAN," he would say defiantly.) He would not wear a girl's bathing suit, opting instead for a t-shirt and shorts. And when we went to get his hair cut before he started kindergarten, he told me, "I want my hair short, like daddy's." So, when Evan was five years old and started saying things like "I want to be a boy" and "when I grow up, I'm going to be a man and marry a woman," we weren't too shocked or concerned. He was happy, he was confident, and because our present culture is more permissive of girls who express themselves in more typically masculine clothes, hair, and activities, our friends and family celebrated his independence and strength. Also, he was only five, and to tell the truth we thought he might just grow out of this. He did not.

When Evan started asking us when he would develop breasts like his older sister because "I don't want them," and saying things like "I'm going to cut my breasts off when I grow up," we started to worry. We didn't want any of our children to hate their body, and any talk of self-mutilation was terrifying. One day I asked Evan, then five years old, "Are you sad you were born a girl?" "Yes, Mommy," he said. "I told God when I was a star in the sky that I was a boy, but God made me a girl and now I just have to live with it."

Nothing in my experience as a parent or as a pastor had prepared me for this conversation, but I deeply believe that God doesn't make mistakes and knew that my child had a profound sense of self-awareness. In that moment, the Spirit placed in my heart the words of Psalm 139: "Before I knit you together in your mother's womb, I knew you...you are fearfully and wonderfully made."

I responded, "Honey, God made you, just as you are. God knows you, inside and out, and loves you, just as you are. Your body is only part of who you are. And did you know there are boys who were born girls and girls who were born boys?" "No, Mommy, that's not true," he replied. (Evan didn't know any transgender people or even that they exist, I realized. He was much too young to have been exposed to transgender issues in popular culture.)

"It's true," I said. "Some people are called 'transgender,' and maybe that's what you are."

So Evan, and my husband, and I started seeing a therapist, and I started looking for positive stories about transgender people that I could share with him, to help him see that transgender people existed and were thriving in the world. I joined a parent-support group and heard other parents' stories of their children's gender journey. Through this group we made friends, and Evan started having occasional playdates with other transgender kids. For the first time he felt safe, knowing the other kids would accept him as a boy who used to be a girl. We told our other children and our extended family, all of whom responded with tremendous love and support. Our church celebrated Evan's new self-identity. Evan socially transitioned at school, changing his name and pronouns in the middle of first grade, and was met with much acceptance there, too.

We were lucky. Our family had resources, a supportive community, and the opportunity to help our child transition without feeling significantly conflicted about our faith or relationships in our community. We didn't have to cut off long-time friendships or change schools or churches. We had supportive doctors, therapists, health insurance.

Yet, to be honest, it still wasn't easy. We grieved the loss of our daughter. Even today, we sometimes still fear for Evan's safety and well-being. We wondered if we were making the right choices. We had had to learn about the transgender experience ourselves and then educate others, becoming advocates for something we initially knew so little about.

When we receive blessings, I believe, it is our responsibility to share those blessings with others. My husband and I and our children have been blessed with support, with acceptance, with community, with wisdom throughout Evan's gender-transition journey. This book is an attempt to share some of those blessings with other parents who are going through the same thing we did but may not have the same sources of support or access to affirmation. I am writing this book for you, so that while you might be grieving or conflicted about your child's gender identity right now, you will know you are not alone. There are lots of parents who have made and are making this same journey with their kids. I am also writing this book so that you might have a resource to share with your friends, extended family, and faith community to help increase the circles of support around you and your child.

I want to honor and offer my deepest gratitude to the families who were willing to be interviewed for this book and who allowed me to share parts of their stories. In the process of writing, I conducted nearly twenty interviews with a very diverse group of parents and kids from across the country who have had widely varying experiences with their children's gender journeys. I also had some very wise parent and transgender friends who read this book in its draft form and offered their valuable insights and suggestions.

Many of the conversations with families were tender, vulnerable, and sometimes painful; unless explicitly stated otherwise, I have changed all their names. But the stories remain true.

Parenting is always a daring adventure; and parenting a transgender or gender-diverse child may be even more so. But there is much that's wonderful about this daring adventure, and I can't wait to share it with you in the pages ahead.

Rachel A. Cornwell
Washington, D.C.
Transgender Day of Remembrance
November 20, 2022

THE LUCKY ONES

Luck always favors the brave.
And you must remember that brave
are the people who follow their heart;
brave are the people who take chances in life.

Preity Zinta
actress and humanitarian

When my husband, Marcus, and I started sharing with others outside our family that our child is transgender, many supportive friends, neighbors, and members of our church and school community would say to us, "Evan is so lucky to have you as parents."

This affirming response has always come from a place of compassion and awareness of how important family support is, especially for LGBTQ+ youth. One national study of transgender and gender non-conforming adults conducted in 2016 showed that rejection from family contributed significantly to their self-harming behaviors. More than 40% said they had attempted suicide at some point in their life, and more than a quarter reported misusing drugs or alcohol as a way of coping with transgender-related discrimination. The greater the experience of rejection, the study showed, the more likely someone was to self-harm.[3] In 2020, the Trevor Project conducted the largest ever national survey of LGBTQ youth mental health, surveying 40,000 LGBTQ youth ages 13-24 across the United States. According to this survey, among youth with high levels of support from family and friends 13% have attempted suicide in the past year, as compared

---

[3] Klein, Augustus and Sarit A. Golub, "Family Rejection as a Predictor of Suicide Attempts and Substance Misuse Among Transgender and Gender Nonconforming Adults," LGBT Health Vol. 3, No. 3, published online: 25 May 2016

with 22% (almost twice as many) of LGBTQ youth with less support.[4]

When Kevin (not his real name) was in seventh grade, he started to experience symptoms of depression and anxiety. Kevin began cutting himself, and he developed an eating disorder due to body dysphoria. His parents were, of course, very worried, and his mother took him to a therapist who gave him a depression-screening survey, which is how his parents discovered that Kevin had been thinking about suicide daily and that he had a plan to take his own life. It was through the process of treating his mental-health issues, Kevin started binding his breasts and wearing boys' clothes, but he still didn't identify as transgender at that time. His parents tried to simply support him and follow his lead as he explored his gender identity. Five years later, Kevin's the most mentally healthy and stable he's ever been, and he's thriving.

Kevin is one of the lucky ones who had the support of family and a caring mental health professional who affirmed his gender identity and helped him work through his depression and gender dysphoria with care and compassion.

---

[4] The Trevor Project, National Survey on LGBTQ Youth Mental Health, 2020 https://www.thetrevorproject.org/survey-2020

⌐

As most of us probably know from our own experiences, adolescence is an unsettling time of life. But it can be especially so for those struggling with their sexuality or gender identity, especially those who are rejected, bullied, harassed, vulnerable, and/or isolated. Too many LGBTQ youth are struggling alone and hiding their true selves rather than living their truth, growing, and thriving. Which is why those kids who are part of an affirming family, who have parents who love and accept them and are willing to learn how to support them in their transition, are the lucky ones

But gender-diverse kids should not have to depend on luck to survive. It should not be left up to chance for a transgender kid's well-being to be dependent on living in the right community or with the right family; belonging to the right church, synagogue, mosque, or temple; or having the right friends and resources to seek support and care they need. These things should be a basic right, a fundamental experience, a baseline that transgender and gender-diverse kids have. Period. Full stop.

If you are the parent of a transgender, non-binary, or gender-diverse child struggling with this new reality— this change in expectations in what you thought your or your child's life would be like—you may not *feel* lucky. Maybe your child's gender transition has come as a surprise to you, and you feel as if you have done something wrong or failed in some way. Perhaps your gender-diverse or transgender child is unhappy, depressed, confused, angry, and you seriously fear for their safety and well-being. But I can assure you, although it will not always feel that way, especially when your kids are hurting, that *we*—the parents and families of gender-diverse kids—*really are the lucky ones.*

I admit my husband and I haven't always felt lucky to be the parents of a transgender child. But with time, as we listened to and learned more from our kid and the experiences of other parents and watched Evan grow more fully into himself and be so happy living his life as a boy, we came to realize how lucky we really are. Now that Evan is in middle school, we can see that our son knew clearly who he was at a young age. We are fortunate that he felt and still feels safe enough to tell us so we have been able support him. We are blessed to have an extended family that, by and large, supports and embraces Evan for who he is, unconditionally.

- We live in a community that is open minded and progressive around LGBTQ concerns and issues.
- We have a school that has been willing to work with us to support our child and his transition.
- Most people we know are willing to be educated.

+ We are part of a church that loves our son and our family and provides a place where Evan can be himself and where we hear from the pulpit grace and mercy and love for all, and not condemnation and judgement and hate-speech.
+ We live in a metro area where there are medical professionals, mental health resources, and even a children's hospital with a whole department dedicated to gender development.
+ We have health insurance that covers us when we seek mental health and medical care for our son.
+ We have an extended community, in person and online, of other parents of transgender children so our son has peers and friends.
+ And as parents, we support and receive support from other moms and dads and grandparents who are also on this same journey with kids who are exploring their gender identities in diverse and multitudinous ways.

Like I said, we are lucky in so many ways. You can be too. It begins with making the decision to love and accept your child for who they are and are becoming, and making a commitment to learn along with them and from them, too.

⌐⁓

Caitlin Ryan is a clinical social worker and director of the Family Acceptance Project at San Francisco State University. She has worked on LGBTQ health and mental health for 40 years, focusing on preventing risk and promoting well-being for LGBTQ children and adolescents. The Family Acceptance Project (FAP) has developed a family support model that helps families learn to support their LGBTQ children by meeting them where they are at. FAP shows families that some of the behaviors they thought were helping their LGBTQ child can contribute to higher risks for health problems and family conflict. Using compassion, culturally grounded education, counseling, and behavioral work, FAP has helped families decrease rejection, increase support, and change outcomes for their children. Ryan writes:

> Families can learn to support their LGBTQ children when guidance and services are provided in ways that resonate for them, including education presented in the context of cultural and religious values. Supporting our LGBTQ and gender-diverse children is not just about protecting them from harm. It's about promoting their well-being, developing their strengths and abilities and, most importantly, helping their families accept and nurture them.[5]

---

[5] "Parents don't have to choose between their faith and their LGBT kids," Caitlin Ryan, Religion News Service, January 7, 2015

For us as parents, we must remember this: Gender identity is not a choice for our kids. It is who they are; it is who God made them to be. There was nothing Marcus and I did to "make" Evan transgender, and there's nothing we could or should have done to keep him from being transgender.

These eye-and-heart-opening journeys with our kids are usually an unexpected detour for most of us, and it's not always easy. There is a lot we parents have to learn—not only so we can understand our own child, but also so we can help them navigate complicated social systems like school, friendships, medical care, politics, work, and their spiritual development. There are fears and worries and grief, as well. You may feel like saying, "I didn't ask for this! This is not what I expected my parenting journey to be like!"

But the truth is that all parenting is much like this, isn't it? When we see that first grainy, black-and-white sonogram picture or finally get that adoption letter, we start envisioning how our lives will change. We might paint the nursery blue or pink or a neutral color. We choose a name and dream what our child's life is going to be like. There are lots of things that we hope for us and for our kids. But there is always more to our amazing journey than we could never imagine.

And when changes, revelations, and surprises come, we adapt as parents. Thank God for that ability! We learn new things, develop different skills, and seek support for our children, and most likely ourselves.

~

When Evan started to transition in first grade, he was already involved in Girl Scouts. His older brother, however, was a Cub Scout. As a Daisy, Evan would go to meetings where the Girl Scouts sat in a circle and talked about things. They made friendship bracelets and sold cookies and went on short hikes, mostly along paved paths. But Graham's Cub Scout den went on campouts where they built campfires and got dirty; they raced Pinewood Derby cars and learned how to use a pocketknife. Evan told us one day that he didn't want to be a Girl Scout, he wanted to be a Boy Scout, he said, because "the girls just sit around and talk about being friends but the boys go on *daring adventures!*" Now, as a Girl Scout leader myself, I knew this wasn't totally accurate. We had done some pretty fun *and* adventurous things with my older daughter's troop! But I got Evan's point: He wanted to do the things he saw boys doing, not the things that the girls his age were doing. It was another way that he was trying to tell us, "I'm a boy, not a girl."

Since Evan started exploring his gender, our whole family has been on a daring adventure together. Embracing this journey as a new and exciting experience has helped us stay open to the unexpected, invited us to learn and grow, and come to understand how truly lucky we are.

QUESTIONS FOR REFLECTION AND DISCUSSION FOR PARENTS

1. What are some things others feel are burdens but you consider "lucky" for you and your family? Be specific. Where does that optimism come from? Tell a story.

2. What are some of the things you have noticed about your child or children that indicate to you that their gender identity is fluid or not fully formed? How do you react to those things, positively or negatively? How do you want to react? How will you work to change your responses to be more sensitive?

3. Do some online research on famous people who were/are members of the LGBTQ+ community. Work their stories into your examples of the kinds of people you hope your children will become.

CHOICES

We don't get to choose what is true.
We only get to choose what we do about it.

Kami Garcia
Beautiful Darkness

CHOICES

Let's call her Leah. When Leah was born, everyone assumed she was a boy because of how her body looked. But as she grew into a toddler, she loved princesses, fairies, and gravitated towards the girls in preschool. When she turned three, Leah asked her parents for a "Frozen" movie-themed birthday party. They agreed, but they were so nervous about how other kids would react they didn't invite any of Leah's friends and just had the party at home with family members. That Christmas, Leah's parents took her to visit Santa at the mall, and when she sat on his lap she told him, "All I want for Christmas is an Elsa dress." But just as her parents feared, the jolly old elf laughed at this child who looked like a boy and wanted to dress up like a princess.

When Leah went to kindergarten, this happy, free-spirited child began to shut down emotionally. Elementary school, it turned out, was a much more gendered place than she had experienced in her young life, and the expectations around gender expression—what clothes kids wear, whom you play with, and what types of activities are "for girls" and "for boys"—was more clearly delineated than in preschool. Leah started to become more aware that her emerging gender identity was something that other kids and adults did not approve of.

Because of the established gender roles of this new environment, Leah didn't want to go to school or even leave the house. She was angry much of the time. She was told that she couldn't be a Daisy Scout like her girlfriends, because everyone saw her as a boy. She was devastated.

Leah's mom, Hannah, had known there was something different about her child from early on. She and Leah went to a therapist and then to a hospital that had a gender clinic for children and youth. The therapist suggested that an upcoming family trip out of the country for Thanksgiving could be a safe time for Leah to try some new clothes. They packed a few dresses, skirts, and sparkly tops, and while on this family adventure, Mom saw her child free and happy for the first time in a long time. And when they came home, Hannah knew she couldn't make her beautiful child identify as male any longer.

Leah wanted to socially transition, to start dressing like a girl and using female pronouns outside their house. Hannah found the book *Phoenix Goes to School* by Michelle Finch, a children's book about a transgender girl who is preparing for her first day of school, excited but also scared of being bullied because of her gender identity. *My Mommy tells me I'm perfect and to be brave* Phoenix says to herself. *You know who you are. Just be yourself, and always listen to your heart.*

When Hannah read this book to her daughter, it made the mother cry, a cry of release from all the emotions she was feeling about her child's transition. But despite Hannah's tears, Leah knew that her mom supported her. And so the next day she went to school and told her teacher "My mommy cried because she's proud of me." That year, Leah's teacher had chosen for the classroom theme "show your true colors." And with the support of her family and school community, this is exactly what Leah began to do.

Hannah had grown up in the Catholic Church, and her faith had taught her that, "God wouldn't want anyone to be anyone but themselves." Even Leah's very religious grandmother was supportive, saying to her granddaughter, "Leah, you should be who you really are."

~

People *should* be who they really are. Here is the hard truth that is difficult for many cisgender people to accept: Being transgender is not a choice. To be transgender is to live according to the gender identity that is the most authentic expression of your true self. It takes courage, honesty, and deep authenticity to be transgender.

It used to be a common assumption that people *choose* to be gay or lesbian, bisexual, nonbinary, asexual or transgender—and some people still believe this to be true. But science has shown that while sexual orientation and romantic attraction is complex, and while there are many factors that shape a person's sexual feelings, it is fundamentally *not* a choice that someone makes. It is something deeply inherent to each person's identity.

How do I know this? I know it because of children like Evan and Leah and so many other young children and youth I have personally known or worked with have convinced me that this is the only way God would have things. People need to be their full, beautiful diverse selves.

We are starting to learn that children do not make a choice to be gender-fluid, non-binary, or transgender.

Their gender identity comes from a deep sense of self, an awareness of the person they are and the gender identity that most fits them. And that who they are is not in alignment with the way in which our culture has labeled them. For example, my friend Sylvia—not her real name—is the parent of a non-binary teenager, and part of what helped her to more easily accept her child's gender transition was recalling her own group of friends in high school. At that time, she identified as a "tomboy," and among the friends she naturally gravitated towards were those whose gender identity or sexuality didn't neatly fit into the categories of straight or gay; whose expressions of self were not limited by the simple binary formula: male or female.

But especially in the 1990s, and in the small community where Sylvia grew up, the language that could have enabled and empowered her and her friends to claim an identity that was "gender fluid" or "non-binary" or "pansexual" simply didn't exist. They knew they were different from most of their classmates, but unlike the kids of today they didn't have the terms to express the ways in which they knew themselves to be different from what is now dubbed the "heteronormative culture."

Because of her own experience as a young woman, Sylvia has helped her child explore their own gender identity in a healthy way, allowing them space to figure themselves out, and it has opened her up to view her own experience in new ways as well.

⌐

Although we broadly assume that how we understand gender is natural and normative, the very idea of gender is fundamentally a social construction. In Western culture, by and large, there have only been two accepted (and acceptable) genders—male and female. And we base the assignment of those genders at birth based upon an infant's physicality—specifically, on genitalia. But there have always been people for whom these binary labels did not fit, for whom "male" or "female" felt limiting or just plain wrong.

As we learn more and there is increasingly greater understanding and acceptance of gender diversity, more and more people are "coming out" as trans or non-binary or asexual or queer, some at younger and younger ages. It is this last issue—age—that has caused so much political and religious consternation. But gender identity is not a fad or a trend. According to Linda Hawkins, Co-Director of the Gender and Sexuality Development Clinic at Children's Hospital in Philadelphia, children begin to have an innate sense of their gender identity between the ages of three and five.[6] Think back to yourself at that age. Do you remember when you realized you were a girl or

---

[6] "When Do Children Develop Their Gender Identity?" by Linda A. Hawkins, PHD, MS.Ed, LPC, Children's Hospital of Philadelphia, https://www.chop.edu/news/health-tip/when-do-children-develop-their-gender-identity

a boy? If you are cisgender, you probably don't, because your assigned gender matched up pretty well with who you knew yourself to be. Your clothes, hairstyle, toys, peer group (most of which were likely strongly influenced by your parents, family, and society at large) fit with who you knew yourself to be, and you were affirmed in that identity without having to think much about it. But for transgender and gender-diverse young people that's not usually the case.

Some children express their gender identity fairly clearly, starting at a young age. Our son, Evan, who had been assigned female at birth, began dressing in clothes that are more commonly identified as boy clothes and cutting his hair short in preschool. This type of expression is not uncommon, but when Evan started kindergarten, he started saying things like "I want to be a boy when I grow up" and "When I grow up, I'm going to be a boy and marry a girl." He was starting to articulate something that wasn't just about how he looked on the outside. It was about how he felt on the inside.

This was before he knew about people who are transgender. But learning about and meeting transgender and gender-non-conforming people was important to him as a child exploring his gender identity. By helping him see that transgender people existed, we were offering Evan a possible way of being in the world that felt right to him.

For a young girl I would like to call Sadie, having a family and a faith community that affirmed her understanding of how God has created human beings has made a huge difference in her life. When she was a young child, Sadie seemed like "a boy who liked girl things." She always gravitated to pink, sparkly things, and loved Barbie dolls. It wasn't until she started seventh grade in a new public school that Sadie first began identifying fully as a girl. And her church, which openly affirms LGBTQ+ persons, celebrated her transition. Right now, *transgender* is not a label that Sadie likes to apply to herself. According to her mom, Annie, "Sadie just likes to be accepted as a girl, and she just wants to be identified as who she really is. She doesn't want to be a transgender poster-child." But, because Sadie knows that people in her family, her school, and her church affirm her transgender identity and see *all* of who she is, she has a positive sense of her own self-worth and well-being as a seventh-grade girl.

A couple I am choosing to call Dan and Holly are parents of a transgender teen who live in a rural and predominantly conservative community. Holly says, "People in our part of the state say that we shouldn't show trans people on TV or allow kids to be exposed to the 'gay lifestyle' for their own protection. As if seeing someone who is gay or trans will make someone into something they aren't. But what if these kids see themselves represented or reflected in the culture? Maybe that helps them come into an understanding of who they are more easily."

While there are many gifts to being trans, there are also daily struggles around so many of the things those who are cisgender take for granted, like feeling safe using a public restroom, accessing health care, or even just finding clothes that fit. Trans and gender-diverse people face constant reminders in our binary culture that they are outsiders. The language we use, the way we create physical space, the ideals of beauty and athleticism, and roles in relationships are all places where transgender people have to make their own way, and so many of these things are so embedded in our culture and the way things work that we don't even see it much of the time.

People who don't understand the journey of a gender-diverse child will sometimes say things like, "I won't let my child choose what we're having for dinner most days, because all we would eat is pizza and chicken nuggets. How can you let your child choose something as serious as their gender?"

In response to these types of comments, I like to ask: If your child said that they were afraid of the dark, if they were having nightmares about things in their closet or under the bed, if they screamed out in the night, you would help them, wouldn't you? You would give them a nightlight, create bedtime rituals; you would get out of your bed and comfort them until they could sleep again. Even if you didn't believe in the monsters, you would trust your child's fear as something real, wouldn't you?

Or if children say they feel sick or tell you that their stomach or head hurt, you don't ignore them or tell them to just forget about it. Even if there doesn't seem to be anything wrong with them—no fever or vomiting or any discernible signs of an illness—you take it seriously, don't you?

Or if children say they want to be an astronaut when they grow up and draw pictures of themselves aboard rockets, dressed up in a space suit, and watch endless YouTube videos about space exploration, you'd pay attention, wouldn't you? You would support their passion, get them books about space from the library, maybe even send them to space camp. You would paint planets on the ceiling of their bedroom and encourage them to shoot for the stars.

These analogies aren't perfect, but they capture some of what it's like to be the supportive parent of a child exploring or questioning their gender identity. Along this journey, there will be days filled with anxiety and worry; but there will also be moments of joy and pride when you see how clearly children know who they are meant to be.

QUESTIONS FOR REFLECTION AND DISCUSSION BY PARENTS

1. Do your children feel comfortable sharing with you questions they have about gender and sex? If so, how do you respond and, if not, what might you want to do differently?

2. Do you think gender and sexual identity are a choice? What is your answer based on? How does it affect how to relate to your child? Are you open to the idea that gender and sexual identity may not be a choice and, if so, how would that change how you relate to your child?

3. What are three things your child is most passionate about. Are each a "male" or a "female" or a "neutral" interest? Why do you think you assigned these genders to these interests?

GO WITH THE FLOW

A tree that is unbending is easily broken.

Lao Tzu

When my husband, Marcus, and I were expecting our first child, at our twenty-week sonogram—once we were assured that our baby was healthy and developing normally—the technician asked if we wanted to know the sex of our baby. "No, don't tell us," I said, "we want to be surprised." A few months later, our baby was born with female genitalia and assigned a gender—a girl! We had tried to keep everything pretty gender-neutral up to that point, filling our baby registry with onesies and sleepers in light greens and yellows. The walls of the nursery were a pale purple with blue-and-white clouds on the ceiling. We were gifted with board books and developmental toys, appropriate for a baby, regardless of gender. But as soon as our daughter, Nora, was born and identified as a girl, it felt like everything changed. Friends, relatives, and sweet, sweet church people showered her in pink. She received baby dolls and frilly dresses and hairbows (even though she was practically bald until well after her first birthday).

With our second child, Graham, we opted to find out the sex before the baby was born, and because he had male anatomy, he was announced to be a boy. And he still identifies that way at age 14. (He, of course, got the full-blue approach to décor and clothing.)

It wasn't until our third child, Evan, was born that we actually got our surprise. While our second child, four at the time, insisted that the bump in my midsection was not a baby but a firetruck, we had a healthy baby who was assigned female at birth but later told us that he was a boy. "I'm a boy in my heart and in my head," was how Evan put it.

⌒

We always have and still try to raise all our kids with a sense that nothing is off limits to them because of their gender, that they should be free to identify and express themselves in whatever way feels true for them. So Graham now has long hair and pierced ears; Nora is an aspiring scientist. But starting from their very first moments outside the womb, nearly everything in our culture has been at work on both of them, trying to reinforce the male/female gender binary that is so prevalent in our culture. From clothes to toys to sports—even things that have no need to be gendered–often are: princess pull-ups for girls and bedspreads that are covered with vehicles for boys, fast-food kids' meals that are designated "for boys" or "for girls," and on and on. The pressure to conform to binary-gender norms is relentless.

The truth is that gender is a social construct, and gender identity is, and always has been, on a spectrum, meaning that in human experience there is a wide range of gender expression and identity that is not easily categorized as simply "male" or "female." There are many people who clearly identify with the gender assigned to them at birth and are comfortable with that identity as male or female. We now have a word for that: *cisgender*, which means a person whose gender identity corresponds with the sex assigned to them at birth. But there are also lots of people who identify as male and express themselves in more traditionally feminine ways, and vice versa. There are people who don't identify with either gender, or who identify with both genders at once, or whose gender identity is more fluid in their understanding and expression.

Non-traditional gender identities have been labeled as "outside the norm," but they have always been part of the human experience and are starting to become more accepted. Before Western colonization of Indigenous peoples and the introduction of binary-gender systems with their own specified behaviors, roles, and clothing, gender diversity was widely accepted and celebrated in many cultures around the world.[7] Some signs that things are starting to shift again, towards a wider understanding of gender identity, include the U.S. State Department's decision in 2021 to allow people to use the gender marker with which they identify on their passports, rather than what is printed on a birth certificate, and one of those options includes "non-binary." Even my own United Methodist Church (which has not exactly been a leader on LGBTQ+ inclusiveness) announced that starting in 2022 in the United States, the annual reporting of our demographic data will include non-binary as well as male and female persons in our church membership.

---

[7] Phillips, Thomas. "Gender Diversity Around the World," November 7, 2018 https://lifeintheleaves.blog/2018/11/07/gender-diversity-around-the-world/

As parents, raising children in this shifting landscape of gender identities, we might feel like we still have a lot to learn in order to help our kids discover who they know themselves to be and feel comfortable in their own skin. We may find that our kids have much more fluid ideas around gender identity than we do, and that we are often learning from them. It's an exciting and daunting and confusing and wonderful time to be a parent.

Joan and Sarah are a same-gender couple raising a young child I'm calling Rosie, who identifies as non-binary. Because the family has many gay, lesbian, and trans people in their neighborhood, among their friends, and in their faith community, Joan and Sarah were always very intentional about raising their child to be as open about gender and sexuality as possible. They use gender-non-specific language for people (like "friend" or "child" rather than "boy" or "girl") and interchangeable pronouns for characters in books. They ask Rosie what pronouns their stuffed animals prefer. They are trying to raise their child with an expansive view of gender and sexuality. So it wasn't totally surprising to them when Rosie told them last year that they were not a boy nor were they a girl. Rosie didn't have the language to describe their gender identity until they were reading a book, *It Feels Good to Be Yourself*, by Theresa Thorn and Noah Grigni. When they got to the page about non-binary identity, Rosie's face lit up. "That's me!" Rosie exclaimed.

From the beginning, Joan and Sarah were not deeply invested in their child's female identity, because they don't strongly identify with the gender binary themselves, but it was still hard for Joan to come to the realization that Rosie might one day change their name. It is a name that holds a lot of meaning for her, so Joan is doing her own emotional work to embrace that possible change. "If we don't assume that our kids are all straight and cisgender in the first place," Sarah told me, "then we don't have as much to lose or give up if our child does identify as queer. Joan and I used to tell people who asked that 'our child is a girl, until we are informed otherwise.' But the assigned gender of your kids doesn't change the type of parent you are going to be for them, and I believe that all children benefit from being freed from gendered expectations. If you talk with your kids about trans/non-binary experience and make space for gender difference in your home, it won't make your kids gay or trans, but it will make them more accepting of difference and more kind to everyone."

Just as our children are learning who they are in all kinds of ways as they grow up, they are also living into their true gender identity; and while some children are, from an early age, very clear about their gender identity, others are more fluid. Their process to self-identify can evolve as they figure themselves out. As parents, our primary job is to make space for our children to become fully themselves. And while it is often just part of the process of a young person figuring themselves out, gender fluidity is one reason why critics say that transgender kids are too young to know who they are, because they might change their minds. A child's lack of consistency or clarity around their gender identity may make some parents feel cautious about, or even resistant to, allowing their child to transition. It can be a confusing experience for parents to walk with their child as they experiment with different gender identities and expressions to find what feels right.

Not all kids who experiment with their gender expression are transgender. But kids who are transgender often do know, deep inside, who they are, even from a very young age. According to the American Academy of Pediatrics, around the age of two children become conscious of the physical differences between boys and girls. Before their third birthday most children can easily label themselves as either a boy or a girl, and by age four, most children have a stable sense of their gender identity. This is why some trans and non-binary kids may already know who they are in preschool even if they don't yet have the vocabulary or feel safe to express their true gender. According to the transgender athlete, activist, and educator Shuyler Bailer, "It's true that [young] children do not yet have mature executive functioning but, if anything, that shows how much these kids already know who they are, because they haven't yet fully learned how they are 'supposed' to be."

Most psychological experts say that a child is transgender if they are *consistent, insistent, and persistent* in their gender identity, but not every gender-fluid child is all three of these things, or all three at the same time. Julie and Matt's son, I call him Alex, came out to his parents as transgender when he was twelve years old with a text message. "I really don't know how to tell you this so I'm just going to," he wrote. "I'm trans. I know it's all pretty complicated but I've been wanting to tell you this for a while but I was too scared." Alex had first come out to his parents as lesbian in sixth grade, but a few months later he felt that bisexual was more accurate to describe his sexuality. And then he experienced gender dysphoria, which led him to understand himself to be transgender.

For Alex's dad, Matt, who is an Episcopal priest, and his mother, Julie, who is a church musician, their child's sexual orientation wasn't a surprise or even an issue. But the idea of gender transition was different. For his parents, the announcement that Alex is transgender felt like it came out of the blue, but for Alex it was something he had apparently been wrestling with for years. Wanting to support their child and ease his anxiety, the family went shopping for more gender-appropriate clothes right away and got Alex's hair cut short. They talked about it with a therapist and doctors.

Alex's parents wanted to approach this change gradually, but it was all too slow for Alex. It took Julie and Matt a while to call Alex by that name, for example, which frustrated Alex, who felt like his parents weren't trying hard enough. Like lots of teenagers, transgender teenagers can sometimes feel like their parents *just don't get it*, even when they are trying. But now, two and a half years later, Alex has started cross-hormone therapy. He now identifies as transgender/non-binary and uses both he/him and they/them pronouns. His parents are supportive, but they admit that they are also still processing their own emotions associated with these changes. Mostly, they are trying to go with the flow and follow their young-adult child's lead as his own process of self-discovery unfolds.

My point is this: It isn't always easy for us parents and siblings and other family members, and yet just because it's hard doesn't mean we should not continue to explore this path along with our child. "In our world, dear reader, sad and terrible things often happen, though I wish I could tell you otherwise. But strangely wonderful things also occur, and this is the truth that makes life worth living," writes the poet John Mark Green.[8] This daring adventure of gender diversity can be challenging, but it is full of strangely wonderful things, too.

When our son Evan had his initial intake meeting with a psychiatrist at the Gender Development Clinic

---

[8] John Mark Green, *She Had a Very Inconvenient Heart: A Tale of Love and Magic*, 2020

at Children's National Medical Center in Washington, DC, the doctor emphasized to our son that he "didn't have to be a boy; that he could be a girl if he wanted to." I was taken aback by this; I found it confusing because my spouse and I felt like we had already done so much work to transition ourselves: We had grieved our loss of a daughter and embraced our son. The therapist wisely explained to me that Evan had a lot of growing up to do, and that he needed to know that he wasn't locked into one path, but that he had the freedom and support to grow into his emerging gender identity. This made a lot of sense, but it meant that I was going to have to learn to stay open and flexible around my child's gender identity for a long time. For the last five years, Evan has remained clear and consistent that he is a boy, but we know that he's still growing and learning more about himself and the world. So, Marcus and I continue to try and stay open to where this journey may take us and remain steadfast in our love and support.

⌒

Even as it is a joy and relief to see our kids grow into their sense of self, to become confident and happy, that doesn't always happen overnight. There can be doubts and grief and anxiety and feelings of loss all along the way—for our kids as well as for us. Naomi's child, someone I'll call AJ, started to express what her mother called "gender variant" behaviors when he was three years old. Assigned female at birth, AJ started rejecting girl's clothes, asking to cut his hair short, and demanding the ear piercings that his mother had given him as an infant be removed.

For Christmas that year, the only thing AJ wanted was a tool set, and when Naomi would say that her child looked pretty, AJ would correct her, "No, Mama, I'm *handsome*." Her child's gender transition was not at all what Naomi had expected for her parenting journey and, as she worked through her own feelings of loss and worry, it reminded her of the experience of giving birth. "I again tried to support and follow where AJ was leading himself/me/us. It was like LABOR and DELIVERY one more time, only this time I was delivering a boy! You really can't guide this process—just as you can't actually deliver a baby yourself. The baby delivers himself/herself to you. My doula shared that with me: Your kid is guiding the delivery; you just ride along. That is what AJ's transition has felt like to some extent. I have a critical role, but the delivery was not mine."

We parents have hopes, dreams, and expectations for our children that are both acknowledged and unacknowledged, and very few of us expect that our child will one day choose to live as a different gender than the one assigned at birth. Name and pronoun changes, changes to our child's appearance and expression, may trigger feelings of loss or fear. They can be hard for us as parents or caregivers to accept or adjust to initially, and we all make mistakes. As one very wise transgender teen shared in response to their parents messing up their chosen name and pronouns: "Don't apologize all the time, because that puts the burden on your kid to respond and reassure you that they are OK. Just correct yourself and move on." Another parent told me that she and her husband spent months practicing their child's new name and pronouns with each other until it became automatic.

Even when we come to a place of acceptance, however, there can be emotions that come unexpectedly, sometimes when we are well into this journey with our kids. A few years ago, I noticed a new "holiday" on social media in mid-September: National Daughter's Day. Apparently, what started in India as a movement to embrace and empower girls morphed into a chance for parents on social media to brag about our female-identified offspring. When this rolled around one year, I was suddenly seeing the photos of so many of my friends' daughters that it was a surprising trigger for me. I found myself with a complicated mix of feelings: pride for my cisgender daughter and a different kind of pride for my transgender son; but I also felt grief for the daughter I no longer have. So this is what I wrote, for all the parents of trans and non-binary kids, on National Daughter's Day:

> I see you, and I'm sending you lots of love. We have made journeys with our children that we never anticipated. We have been cracked open and had our expectations turned upside down; learned things we never knew we had to know. We have learned to love our child who is new to us, and yet still the same

person deep in their soul. We have lived with fear and anger, but have been opened up to so much love and wonder. We have lost what we thought we knew, and we have gained something even more.

So, celebrate your child today. Surround them with love and support, and claim them unconditionally, whether you call them daughter, son, kiddo. Because, you are doing a great job, my fellow parents of trans and non-binary kids. And I see you.

When your child tells you that they feel they are in the wrong body, if they start acting out or experiencing symptoms of depression or engaging in self-harm due to gender dysphoria, it can feel terrifying or overwhelming. As parents, our first concern is always to make sure our kids are safe, that they have the support they need to work through their own feelings and come into their sense of self with the least amount of trauma possible. With so many of the parents I have spoken to about this, their child's realization that they were transgender came, initially, as a shock, but with perspective most of them realized it was something their child had been wrestling with for a long time. Some parents blamed themselves—wondering if they should have known sooner that their child was struggling with their gender identity, if they could have helped them avoid so much anxiety, suffering, or self-harm. But this is a journey, both for your child and for you, and along the way there may be times when it's not always easy or clear what the right decisions are.

Holly and Dan's child, whom I call Savannah, first started saying that she was gay when she was in third grade. But by middle school, she was interested in dating someone of the opposite sex. However, throughout her early teen years, Savannah's anxiety grew exponentially. She started to engage in self-harm and had to be hospitalized with mental health concerns. In eighth grade, she started to identify as transgender, even preparing a power point presentation to inform her parents about her gender identity and the steps she wanted to take to transition. A year later, however, Savannah felt she was more non-binary than trans-female. Holly and Dan were supportive of their child from the outset, and they themselves had many friends in the LGBTQ community. They found a Presbyterian church with an affirming youth ministry program for their child, and it was in this group that Savannah found true community amongst her peers for the first time. Dan and Holly continued to listen to and love their child, but they saw how much she was wrestling within herself. So when Savannah expressed a desire to start cross-hormone therapy, they were understandably cautious. Given how much Savannah had struggled with her own process of self-discovery, they didn't want to rush into any medical interventions that would be irreversible. They started with testosterone blockers, which had an almost immediate effect on Savannah's mood and self-confidence. This step was not only medically necessary; it provided the confirmation they all needed that Savannah was certain about who she is. By the time she started hormone therapy, everyone was on the same page that this was the right decision.

Over the years, Savannah and her whole family suffered emotionally to get to this place of stability. "She has been on a journey of self-exploration, and how she identified was based on the information she had at that time," Holly explains. "I don't know if she had known that being trans was an option from the beginning whether the process would have been different for her. But maybe some of her suffering could have been lessened."

~

Like Dan and Holly, many parents of trans kids feel that they have made mistakes along the way. Not having access to good information, resources, medical providers, or support systems can leave families adrift. Complicated by mental-health struggles for your child or your own feelings of grief, loss, and anxiety over your child's identity, most parents just do the best they can in the moment. If this is you, please be forgiving of yourself. Just keep loving your child and doing your best. It's natural and normal to have all of your feelings—pride, fear, grief, joy, anger. That's got to be part of the process of *your* transition. I encourage you to find support from trusted friends and/ or family; a support group such as PFLAG (Parents and Friends of Lesbians and Gays—a national organization with local chapters throughout the United States), and a counselor or therapist of your own to help you work through your feelings while continuing to be your child's biggest advocate and cheerleader.

Your child's gender journey may not always be straightforward or clear and, in those times, you must learn to go with the flow. Children grow and learn and figure out who they are in so many ways, and gender identity is just one part of that development. But along the way, the most important thing is assurance that they are loved and supported. What is most going to help them to accept themselves is the knowledge that their family accepts who they are and love them unconditionally. That's what every child needs and deserves, after all.

QUESTIONS FOR REFLECTION AND DISCUSSION BY PARENTS

1. List the many ways you love your child unconditionally. Put the list on your refrigerator door.
2. Look back at photos of your child before they came out to you as transgender. Remind yourself of the ways in which your child is still the same person. What are some of their personality traits, preferences, talents, and gifts that have always been part of who they are? Which make you most proud?
3. What is one thing you could do for yourself that would help you feel better or know what to do next? When are you going to do it?

THE WHOLE FAMILY TRANSITIONS

We may have our differences,
but nothing's more important than family.

Miguel
character in the Disney film Coco

When Catlyn decided to become a parent as a single person, she dreamed of having a daughter. She went through the process of adopting a little girl from China and brought her home when she was about nine months old. However, starting in elementary school, this child, whom I call Jamie, began expressing himself as male. Jamie wore boy's clothes and cut his hair short. When the mother and child came to my church, I was lucky enough to baptize Jamie at eight years old. He decided to wear a suit (and he looked amazing). Later, Jamie came out as transgender, identifying as male and adopting a new name and pronouns.

Jamie's gender transition was hard at first for Catlyn, who had longed for a daughter and had given her child a beloved family first name. But the mom knew that the best way to support her child would be to affirm his gender identity and allow him to transition, and so that's what she did. Because she didn't have a partner at the time, and there were no other siblings in their family, the process of supporting Jamie's gender transition was something shared just between the two of them, and yet it was still challenging.

When a child transitions, it impacts the entire family in many ways. If there are multiple children in the family, siblings may feel confused, sad, or even angry over losing a brother or sister. They may also feel jealous about the additional attention being directed towards their transgender or non-binary sibling. Or they might feel worried about what people outside the family will think. This is why the process of a child's gender transition is something that impacts a whole family.

∼

It happens sometimes that co-parents are not of the same mind about supporting their child's gender transition or how to handle certain aspects of a child's social transition, healthcare, or whom to bring into your circle of support. When our son Evan first began questioning his assigned gender identity, I was initially more open to this exploration than my husband, Marcus. Of course, we both had questions and things we needed to discuss and work through together in order to fully support our child, which we were determined to do.

If parents are divorced and already navigating a challenging relationship, different approaches or attitudes regarding a gender-diverse child can exacerbate an already tense situation. Sometimes co-parents just move at different paces on this journey of understanding and acceptance; other times the differences are irreconcilable. Because the support transgender young people receive from their nuclear family is so incredibly important to their sense of safety, well-being, and being loved, it is important for everyone in the family to acknowledge the ways that the gender journey of a child affects each of them, and to work through this transition together. Helping the whole family transition becomes essential

THE WHOLE FAMILY TRANSITIONS

for extended family, friends, and members of their faith community.

A girl I call Naomi came out as transgender at the age of twelve. She first broached the subject with her mom, and later told her dad via a text message. Naomi's parents had been divorced for a few years already, so Naomi was used to having to communicate with her parents separately. At first, her dad, Nate, was struggling to understand his daughter's transition because he only spent half of each week with her and didn't feel that he had the whole picture. But in sharing information and observations with Naomi's mom, he came to understand that Naomi was coming into her true self.

Still, as time went on, navigating Naomi's transition, her healthcare, and other support systems became challenging because of the fractious relationship between the two parents. Nate recently launched a divorce-coaching program, and his advice for co-parents who may be experiencing conflict related to their child's gender transition is to:

+ Keep the well-being of your child the focus. Discuss what outcome you want for your child and understand the risks of not working together to provide full support as your child explores their gender identity.
+ Seek out a family therapist who has experience with transgender children and youth and

work with that person to navigate differences of perspectives.

+ Share information with each other—what you are noticing about your child's mental, physical, and emotional health. Keep lines of communication open when it comes to your child's well-being.

+ Make sure there is clarity about the process of making decisions regarding your child's healthcare and any medical interventions in which both parents need to be involved.

If you have other children in your household, a sibling's gender transition will most certainly have an impact on them as well. In our family with three wonderful kids, our middle child struggled at first with his brother's gender transition. Graham was eight years old when Evan started to explore his gender identity, and he was at a stage in his own development where the world was very binary and clear cut. "You can't just change your gender," he responded when he was told that we would now be referring to his sibling with male pronouns.

Meanwhile, Nora, our oldest child, then in middle school, was sad and afraid. She was aware of how cruel other kids could be to anyone who was different, and she was also grieving the loss of a sister. We empathized with both these reactions—after all we had experienced some of the same feelings and questions. But we continued to affirm Evan in his gender transition and we reminded all our children that our home was a place where everyone should be able to be themselves and be loved and accepted just as they are. And eventually, with time and the support of a family therapist, everyone in our family came to the same place of acceptance for Evan (and for one another, too).

For most families, when one member transitions it is a process you need to work through together, paying special attention to everyone's unique needs and perspectives. Having a therapist, counselor, or clergy you trust can help your family navigate the conversations and questions and offer the necessary support you need. Gender transition is a "whole family journey," and everyone needs extra love and grace in the midst of it.

"**When my son socially transitioned,** the first people he told outside of our nuclear family was his therapist and then his grandmothers," a mother named Rose told me. "It was really important to him that he had their support." They decided to tell one grandmother first, during a visit at Thanksgiving. The child first asked his mother to tell his grandmother that he now wished to use male pronouns, but the mom knew that her mother would be supportive and wanted her son to have the experience of telling Grandma himself and feeling her love and affirmation in response. At the very last minute of the visit, he pulled his grandmother aside as she was dropping them off curbside at the airport and whispered in her ear. "Grandma, there's something I want to ask you," he began, tentatively, "I want to be called 'he' now. Would you call me 'he'"?

"I could tell he wanted to wait until the moment just before we were to leave, just in case the response from his grandmother was not a positive one," the mom told me. "But thankfully, my mother and I had already talked a lot about his gender journey and she was completely on board."

Although this was a completely new experience for them, both grandparents are open-minded and open-hearted people who love their grandchildren without reservation. They had questions, of course, and worries about what this transition might mean for their grandchild and his future, but they have stood by him and helped form a circle of support around him.

Of course, this is not always the case. Having the support of extended family is a wonderful thing for you and your gender-diverse child. But there can be a lot of reasons why people struggle with acceptance. Sometimes they fear things they don't know or understand. Other times they have heard stories that are false or misleading about transgender people. Perhaps part of the message they have received from their faith community is that being transgender is not acceptable to God. And while it's true that people can change and become open, not everyone will be able to be supportive.

Which is why whom to trust with the experience of your child's gender journey can be one of the most difficult things to decide as you seek to protect your child's well-being. Depending on the age of your child, you may have to follow their lead as to whom they want to be "out" and allow them to take the initiative. And, unfortunately, there may be times when you may need to limit contact with some extended family members for the sake of your child. And that can be really painful for all involved.

Brenda and Ronald are the parents of a non-binary teen I'm calling Aaron, who is out at home and at school but not with extended family. It was a tricky thing for Brenda to navigate with her siblings and mother—using one name and pronouns for her child with her extended family and other names and pronouns with people who knew about their child's gender-identity journey.

Brenda was pretty sure that her extended family would not understand or be accepting of Aaron's gender transition, so she had to keep it to herself, and this was something that created considerable distance between her and people she loved. Brenda and Ronald decided to focus their energy on providing a safe, supportive place at home for Aaron and, when they did, they found that their child was able to have the confidence to advocate for themselves, emailing their teachers to inform them of their name and pronouns, seeking out a group of friends who are mainly LGBTQ+, and creating their own community of friends and chosen family. Aaron eventually has come out to a few extended family members, but not to others.

When I asked Brenda what advice she had for other parents of trans and non-binary kids, she said they should seek out safe, supportive places for themselves as well, groups such as Parents and Friends of Lesbians and Gays (PFLAG), and "kick to the curb" anyone who isn't supportive. "Being part of my nuclear family's inner circle is a privilege," she said. "I would ask other parents of a trans or gender-fluid child to consider why they are keeping homophobic relatives in their inner circle or staying in a faith community that doesn't fully support and affirm their kid."

Of course, that is easier said than done, as Brenda herself would acknowledge. It's hard to feel that you are in a place of having to choose between loving and supporting your child and relationships with friends and family who are not (yet) ready to be supportive. And people can surprise us, too. Sometimes the experience of loving someone who is struggling with or in the process of changing their gender identity, especially a child, can open people's eyes and heart to the experience of being transgender and enable them to join in the joys and struggles of that experience.

For example, Peter's in-laws are immigrants with a strict Muslim background, and he was not at all sure if they would accept his son's gender transition from female to male. Peter and his son, whom I am calling Nader, had many conversations with his grandparents about their grandchild's gender journey leading up to a family wedding where everyone would be together. But when Nader came to the wedding dressed in traditional men's clothing from their Muslim culture, the in-laws, including Nader's grandparents, were surprisingly supportive.

Sometimes we parents and our children just have to tell our story and hope that others *we* love will see the person that *they* love, rather than react to an issue or idea they don't comprehend or think they object to.

QUESTIONS FOR REFLECTION AND DISCUSSION FOR PARENTS

1. Who have been the most difficult relatives or friends you have had to deal with or fear having to deal with regarding your child's transition? Why do you think this is so? Schedule a meeting with a professional counselor to explore the reasons for this difficulty or fear and design a plan for moving forward. Be sure to involve your child in these discussions and decisions.

2. Ask your child what he/she/they want to do about communicating with their relatives, friends, or members of your faith community about their transition. Follow their lead, but also participate with them in making the decisions.

3. Why do you think there is so much discrimination and hatred of trans people right now in our society? What can you as a family do to help change minds and hearts?

SCHOOLS, SEX ED, SLEEPOVERS, AND MORE

*All advocacy is, at its core,
an exercise in empathy.*

Samantha Power
former U.S. Ambassador to the United Nations

Beyond your nuclear and extended family, school is often the next space you will need to navigate with your gender-diverse child. While in some places, schools have become a battleground over transgender issues, it is still possible for school to be a safe and affirming space for gender-diverse kids. Other students, teachers, administrators, and support staff can potentially be great sources of support for your child, but it may require education and advocacy from you, perhaps along with your child, to make sure that school is a safe place in providing the support your child needs.

Gavin Grimm was one of the first openly transgender high school students in the United States. His advocacy helped bring attention to the need for more inclusive schools. When he was barred from using the boy's bathroom at Gloucester High School in Virginia in 2014, his parents sued the school system and won. In the summer of 2021, the Supreme Court refused to take up the case, allowing the lower court ruling—in favor of Gavin being able to use the bathroom that corresponds with his gender identity—to stand. He wrote:

> Now over six years and several court decisions later, the Supreme Court has finally affirmed what should have been a simple request to live like any other kid… at last my victory feels final. But I shouldn't have had to fight this hard. Being a teenager is never easy, especially when society has rejected you almost from the day you were born. I'd always faced bullying and

harassment at school, but it got worse right as I was getting a taste of what it felt like to be comfortable, to be seen, to love myself. I wish my case had been resolved years ago, while I was still in school. It's been challenging fighting in court just to be me. Other trans youth shouldn't have to fight this hard.

Thankfully, things are changing. I've grown up with this case, and the country has as well. More people today say they know someone who is transgender than they did in 2014. More trans youth can say they have a supportive teacher or parent—a crucial factor in reducing rates of depression and suicide among trans kids. But the work of advocates for trans justice is far from over.[9]

As a parent, you may have already experienced having to advocate for your child in a school setting. Whether a child has learning challenges, disabilities, health concerns, or identifies as transgender or non-binary, part of our job as parents is to help the school understand what our child needs to feel safe and be able to learn.

For example, when Monique's son, whom I call Jorge, was diagnosed with serious learning differences,

---

[9] Gavin Grimm, "I Fought for Years in Court for My Basic Rights as a Trans Kid. It Shouldn't Have Been This Hard," *Washington Post* opinion page, June 30, 2021

including dyslexia and ADHD, she knew she would have to advocate within the school for extra resources to help him learn. This experience of advocating for Jorge's learning support gave Monique skills and tools that she relied upon when Jorge later came out as transgender.

However, a significant difference between, say, working with your child's school to get an Individualized Education Plan (IEP) or more educational resources for your school, as opposed to dealing with issues of gender identity, is that your school may never have had a known transgender or non-binary student before. You might not find the same level of acceptance and understanding from school staff as you did with the IEP, or they may not have or know about the resources needed to support your child in their gender transformation journey.

In one family's experience, they had no issues with their child socially transitioning at school. Teachers, administrators, school staff, other students and their parents made the change to using new pronouns and a new name fairly easily; however, changing the official records in the school database was a more involved process. "Although he was now going by a new name and pronouns at school," said Matthew, who is the parent of a transgender elementary student, "all official correspondence that came home was addressed with his 'dead' name, and whenever there was a substitute teacher in his classroom or he purchased lunch in the cafeteria he was misgendered, and this was causing him great anxiety. We knew that we needed to get this changed, but we didn't know the steps to take."

The family didn't really know where to start. Would they have to first change this information on his birth certificate, which they had not done and weren't sure they were ready to do? Would it take time and money and the services of a lawyer? How public would they need to be in order to advocate for their child? They started by contacting the school administration but, because the school had never encountered this situation before, they didn't know the process to change his name or gender markers in the school system or even if it could be done.

Finally, they reached out to their support group of gender-diverse parents at their church for advice and learned from others who had been through the process in another school in the same district that a doctor or therapist's letter affirming that their son identified as male would be sufficient to change the records in the district system. Because they were the first family at their school to request this change, they had to do their own research and then inform the school of what needed to be done. In this case, the process to change the student's name was relatively simple, but it is not always this easy, depending on your school district or even the individual school.

As parents, we have to be ready to take on the role of advocate and educator in our child's school, which can be especially challenging when we are parenting teens who often don't want their parents involved at school and yet need advocates because the experiences of bullying and harassment can be so much worse in middle school and high school than in the lower grades.

One thing that can really help middle-and-high-school-aged transgender students is the presence of a Gender-Sexuality Alliance or Gay-Straight Alliance (GSA) at the school. Even if your child doesn't participate in the GSA, just knowing it is there can be helpful to them in seeking a safe and supportive environment. If there isn't a GSA at your school, it may be a matter of finding a staff person who can serve as a sponsor or asking the parent-teacher association in the school to set aside some funds to create this group.

The Parent-Teacher Association (PTA), sometimes called the Parent-Teacher-Student Association (PTSA), at your child's school can also be a helpful starting place to learn what kinds of policies are already in place and figure out what changes still need to be made. PTAs can also be a resource to help organize informational sessions for parents, students, and school staff. You may want to inquire as to the type of training that staff have received on gender identity and if additional training is needed. Both PFLAG (Parents and Friends of Lesbian and Gays) and the Human Rights Campaign have tool kits for creating more welcoming and safe public schools.[10] While not all schools will be open to engaging in this type of programming, PTAs can sometimes offer trainings on a

---

[10] https://pflag.org/publication/toptenwaystomakeschoolssafe

voluntary basis to staff. This is yet another reason why being involved in your school's PTA is really important.

⌐

Beginning in late elementary school, most public-school districts start to offer some form of sexual health education that usually covers basic information about how the body changes during puberty, social-emotional development, and substance abuse. What is taught in school health curriculum varies widely state to state and school district to school district, so taking advantage of any parent information sessions and viewing the curriculum is important so you can decide whether or not to have your child participate (if the sessions are optional) and/or help prepare your child for the information they will receive.

You may want to ask your child's teacher if students are separated by gender for instruction and, if so, how they will accommodate non-binary students. While sex education is generally an uncomfortable experience for all students, it can be traumatic for transgender and non-binary youth. Spending some time learning about the information that is being presented and preparing your child for this experience can be really important.

Sexual health and sex education is essential for all youth, including transgender and non-binary youth, but school is not the only place where you can access these resources. The Unitarian Universalists and United Church of Christ have created an excellent sex education course for ages five through adult that includes and affirms gender identity and sexual orientation, called *Our Whole Lives (OWL)*. The Unitarian Universalist webpage states, "*Our Whole Lives* provides accurate, developmentally appropriate information about a range of topics, including relationships, gender identity and expression, sexual orientation, sexual health, and cultural influences on sexuality."[11] There is likely a congregation near you that offers OWL, and it may be a good alternative to your school's health education curriculum.

⌒

Supporting the social well-being of your transgender or gender-diverse child is critically important, and friendships are a big part of that at every age and every stage of childhood development. When kids are younger, it's easier for parents to choose their friends and be aware of the ideology and values of our children's friends' parents. At this age, we may need to seek out opportunities for younger children to form relationships with other transgender and gender-diverse peers.

When our son Evan transitioned in first grade, for example, he said to me, "Mom, I am the only kid in my school who is transgender!" I didn't know if this was true or not, but it was how he felt. And I knew that he needed to meet some other transgender youth. Through a local

---

[11] https://www.uua.org/re/owl

parent group for gender-diverse kids, we met three families we really connected with. We started having playdates and even went to a swim party at one family's house. There were about twenty kids and youth there, and Evan played and swam and ate hotdogs. As we were leaving, I asked him if he had a good time. He told me it was so nice just to be able to relax and be his full self. He didn't have to hide anything about himself in this group of people. The kids didn't really spend any time talking to one another about their experience of being transgender (they were too busy having fun). But knowing that everyone there was like him made our son feel safe. And this enabled him to have the confidence to enter into other spaces where he was most likely one of a few, if not the only, transgender kid.

Because your child will likely spend most of their time with kids who are not transgender, when they are younger it's especially important to be aware of families that might not be accepting of your transgender child. As children get older and have more autonomy and independence when it comes to choosing friends, our role as parents shifts to helping them find friends who will be accepting and affirming, even if our child does not disclose their transgender identity to their peers. Just as you would with a cisgender child, it's important to know whom your children are spending time with socially and what the views of these kids and their families are with regard to transgender people.

Older elementary-and-middle-school kids may be invited for sleepovers at the homes of their friends and, especially in these situations, parents have a right to know that their child will be safe in another family's home. You do not necessarily need to disclose your child's transgender identity, unless you know the family well and feel that they will be supportive. You will want to have conversations with your child about specific arrangements, such as where they will change clothes and where they will sleep and what to do if they encounter a situation that makes them uncomfortable (such as having the option to call you and come home, perhaps with no questions asked).

In an article in *Parent's Magazine* entitled "Sleepovers in an Age of Gender Diversity: The Parent's Guide," Amber Leventry recommends having open conversations with your teenager about expectations when it comes to sleepovers. Quoting sex educator Kim Cavill, Leventry suggests asking questions of your child such as: *What kinds of privacy do you think you're entitled to when you have people sleep over?* "This is a good way to invite tweens and teens into conversations about rules, which increases the likelihood of their cooperation and decreases their defensiveness."[12]

As your kids get older, they will hopefully find a peer group that includes other gender-diverse and queer

---

[12] Leventry, Amber, "Sleepovers in an Age of Gender Diversity: The Parents Guide," *Parents Magazine*, October 4, 2019 https://www.parents.com/kids/teens/party/updating-the-sleepover-rules-how-to-talk-to-kids-about-gender-diverse-sleepovers/

kids, as well as straight, cisgender peers. As your direct influence on your child's friend group wanes, one way you can still provide guidance and support is by making your home a safe space for your teen and their friends to gather together. One parent of a non-binary teen, Jeannie, said that she did everything she could to make sure that her house would be the place where her child and their friends would want to hang out. "Our home is a safe space for everyone, where people get to use the names and pronouns they want to use and they get to be normal kids—play video games and ride bikes and go to buy junk food. I feel honored that our home can be a place where my child and his friends can be themselves."

Basically, most transgender kids just want to be like their peers. So whatever you can do to help normalize social situations early on, empower your child to set appropriate boundaries for themselves, and become their own advocate will help them navigate rapidly changing and complex social spaces.

⌒

Another adolescent rite of passage for many kids is summer camp. Camp can be a great experience for all kids—a chance to gain independence, form fast friendships, and experience freedom in being away from home in a safe, supportive environment. But not all camps are equipped to welcome transgender and gender-diverse youth, and it's important to know that your child will be safe and supported before dropping them off for a week or more away from home. On a 2019 episode of the podcast "Nancy," Kathy Tu talked about her experience going to A-Camp, an experience designed for adult queer women and gender non-binary folks, many of whom missed out on the experience of camp as kids.[13] Kathy interviews one camper, Elizabeth, who says, "...a lot of the activities are things you would've done as a teenager or a child at summer camp. Which I think is really appropriate because I think a lot of us here have this sense of not having the childhood that we wanted because we couldn't be out and totally be ourselves, so this is kind of reclaiming a lost queer childhood, I think, for me, and maybe for other people."

Fortunately, this doesn't have to be the case for our kids today. There are several wonderful sleepaway camps that specifically serve LGBTQ youth. Brave Trails Camp, which has locations in Maryland and California, is a leadership focused, overnight summer camp for LGBTQ+ youth ages 12-18; Camp Aranu'tiq in New Hampshire offers a family camp for youth of all ages and their families. The camp song at Aranu'tiq expresses well how summer camp experience should be: "This harbor is safe, this harbor is warm, this harbor is where I can weather a storm. This harbor begins and ends with you and me and there's no place I'd rather be." PFLAG's website has an extensive list of summer camps that offer a safe and nurturing

---

[13] https://www.wnycstudios.org/podcasts/nancy/episodes/nancy-podcast-kathy-goes-to-queer-camp

environment for LGBTQ+ kids, located throughout the United States.[14] And many of these camps also offer financial aid on a first come-first served basis.

In addition to camps whose mission is specifically to serve LGBTQ+ youth, there are summer camps, both secular and faith-based, that are open and affirming to trans and gender-diverse youth. Several families I interviewed spoke about how important these summer camps were in helping their kids to be fully themselves in those spaces. From an Episcopal summer camp in Louisiana that created a gender-neutral cabin, to a Presbyterian camp in Arkansas that welcomed and celebrated a transgender girl, to a United Methodist camp in Maryland where nearly the entire middle-school group was LGBTQ+, many summer camps are places of safety and joy for our kids. It can require a bit of research and talking to camp directors to make sure that they are prepared to welcome and support transgender kids, but sleepaway camp can be a life-changing experience for all kids, and there is no reason why our transgender and non-binary children should miss out on this experience either.

⌒

The participation of transgender youth in sports has become a flash point in the culture wars of late. Because many sports are still segregated by gender, allowing transgender

---

[14] https://pflag.org/youthcamps

kids (especially girls) to play sports on teams that align with their gender identity has recently become a fraught political issue. Advocates for girls' sports have pushed back against trans girls playing on girls' teams because they are "biologically male" and therefore may have a physical advantage. The NCAA swimmer, Lia Thomas, is a recent prominent example of the harsh scrutiny that transgender athletes are subjected to when they compete at an elite level. At the same time, there are starting to be more trans and non-binary role models in professional sports, including Layshia Clarnedon, a non-binary basketball player for the New York Liberty (WNBA); Quinn, a non-binary mid-fielder for the OL Reign, a National Women's Soccer League team; and Rach McBride, a non-binary professional triathlete.[15]

But the reality is that the debate about whether or not to allow transgender youth to play on teams that align with their gender identity is ridiculously overblown. We know that kids of all genders develop at different rates, and most pre-pubescent kids are physically equal, regardless of biological sex. Transgender kids are already at higher risk for mental health issues, and keeping them from participation in sports only denies them access to the proven benefits that physical fitness can have for their self-esteem and mental health. It's also true that being part of a team is important for kids' social development;

---

[15] https://www.si.com/wnba/2021/04/16/nonbinary-athletes-transgender-layshia-clarendon-quinn-rach-mcbride-daily-cover

and being encouraged to play a sport allows trans youth to have a relationship with their body that is *not* about their gender identity but *is* about their personal strengths and abilities.

Eli, as I call him, is a ten-year-old soccer player who also identifies as non-binary. When they first started exploring their gender identity, they weren't sure they would be able to continue to play because they were at an age when teams started to move from being co-ed to single-sex. Their parent, Jennifer, who was herself a college soccer player, worked with their local recreational league to form a gender-inclusive team of 10-and-11-year-old kids.

The "Primers," as the team is named, is a group of about half transgender/non-binary kids and half cisgender kids. Some of the transgender kids are playing soccer for the first time because they finally have a team where they can be fully themselves. While their inaugural season record was not outstanding, there is a lot more to this team experience than winning games. According to Jennifer, there is a sense of belonging that surrounds the entire team. Practices are "a big queer party," she said, with older siblings and parents joining in. While other soccer teams focus purely on athletic ability and winning, the Primers is "150% pure joy," Jennifer says. When other players, coaches, or referees have asked questions or been unkind, the parents and Primer coaches have "formed a wall of love" around the kids. The team has a large community of fans that includes a mascot-dog in a transgender pride t-shirt. They were even visited by the local professional soccer team, the Des Moines Menace, who brought pride-themed soccer balls and autographed player cards to encourage and support these young athletes.

This type of team doesn't happen without a lot of parental support and advocacy, but it's so hopeful to know that this experience is possible and has the potential to influence the culture of youth sports more widely. In addition to co-ed team sports, individual-athlete sports may be another option for your child to explore. Sports like cross country, cycling, track and field, and martial arts can sometimes be more open to gender diversity and more welcoming to transgender and non-binary athletes. Like many other areas of our culture, sports are becoming more inclusive, but we still have aways to go, even at the youth level, to make sure our kids feel safe and supported.

In the summer swim league my family belongs to, we received an email regarding a swimmer for another team that we were going to be competing against. That team had a twelve-year-old who was in the process of transitioning from female to male and was competing in the boys' events. But because of his physical development, we were informed, he was going to continue to wear a one piece "girls" swimsuit that covered his torso. The email we received from the coaches was at the request of the other team, alerting us to this swimmer's attire so that everyone would be prepared to be supportive and kind. While I was grateful for this email and for the expectation that this swimmer would be treated with respect and kindness, my heart also went out to him and his family, because he had no choice but to disclose his transgender identity to every team at every pool that summer if he wanted to compete and have some assurance that he would be treated with the same support and respect that should be given to all athletes (and all people!).

In addition to the need for safe space within the bounds of competition, locker rooms are another place in which safety and privacy for all children, but especially transgender kids, need to be guarded. Ensuring that your child's coaches and the parents of other kids are supportive and watching out for your child's safety is yet another place where we parents have to be aware. Sometimes it involves reminding our transgender kids to guard their privacy, or perhaps having them change clothes at home before or after practices or games and avoiding the locker rooms altogether. These are not insurmountable obstacles to your child's participation in sports; they are just additional things to consider and discuss with your child and/or the coaches or other adults who are responsible for ensuring that children can participate along with their peers, if they so choose.

As parents of transgender kids, we may *have* to become advocates for our children to be able to fully participate in sports in a safe and encouraging environment. But if athletics is something your child enjoys, with your support they should be able to pursue their interest and have the same beneficial experiences that other kids often have when playing sports.

QUESTIONS FOR REFLECTION
AND DISCUSSION

1. Make a list of the gender issues regarding schools, camps, and sports that most bother people you talk with. What books or articles do you need to read about these issues first? Then open a dialogue with those who have expressed those concerns to you.

2. What is the role of parents in protecting their kids, and when is it important not to become too overprotective? How do the issues of gender choices change these equations, and why?

3. Should we design youth sports programs mostly for young people who have the talent to play professionally or at least in college, or for the great majority of young people? Discuss your response and its implications.

A SPECTRUM
OF GENDER-
AFFIRMING CARE

A healthy outside starts from the inside.

Robert Urich

actor

Most transgender people, if they have access to resources such as insurance and medical providers, will at some point seek gender-affirming medical care that will enable them to physically transition. This is becoming increasingly common with adolescents as well, which can be necessary and lifesaving but is also controversial in our current political climate in the United States.

A physical transition is any step or steps a person takes to change their physical body to align with their gender identity, often through hormone therapy and/or surgery. The decision to physically transition is not made lightly and in the vast majority of people is done only after someone has lived for a significant amount of time as a transgender person. It is also true that not all transgender people choose to physically transition, and it is very important to state clearly here that gender variance is not a medical or mental health concern that always needs treatment. A diagnosis of gender dysphoria that causes mental or emotional distress can often be eased through treatment, both physical and mental, but not all gender-diverse people experience gender dysphoria.

And there are many transgender people who would choose to physically transition but are unable to do so due to financial constraints, lack of social or familial support, or not having access to medical providers who can offer them the care they seek. Despite a growing number of gender clinics in the United States, they are often overwhelmed with the number of patients and many have long wait lists. Add the current political climate at the time of the writing of this book and you have the makings of a real crisis on this issue.

⁓

The good news is that the views of medical and mental health communities towards gender diversity has changed significantly in the last few decades and there are now many more providers offering care and support to trans-gender people, including children and youth. In January of 2022, the World Health Organization's "International Classification of Diseases" went into effect worldwide, and that document re-classified "gender incongruence" as part of sexual health and not a part of psychology or mental health concerns. This recognition from the global medical community that transgender identity is part of the spec-trum of normal human experience and not an illness or an aberration is an important and welcome change.

Also in 2022, the eighth version of the "Standards of Care for the Health of Transsexual, Transgender, and Gender Nonconforming People" was released by the World Professional Association for Transgender Health (WPATH). This international organization brings together health professionals from around the world to determine the best practices, based on evidence-based care, for supporting the overall health and well-being of transgender people. WPATH explains that "The overall goal of the Standards of Care is to provide clinical guidance for health professionals to assist transsexual, transgender, and gender nonconforming people with safe and effective pathways to achieving lasting personal comfort with their gendered selves in order to maximize their overall health, psychological well-being, and self-fulfillment."

These are both incredibly important resources, not just for medical and mental health professionals, but also for transgender people and the parents of transgender kids and youth to be aware of so we can all advocate for gender-affirming healthcare.

Finding a good mental health provider is an important first step for parents of gender-diverse kids. When a young person is experiencing gender dysphoria, it can be traumatic and scary for everyone. A good psychologist can provide support, information, and guidance about what additional steps your child needs to take to feel comfortable exploring his/her/their gender identity. Sometimes there are other mental health issues that a young person is experiencing, such as depression, anxiety, eating disorders, or self-harm, which may or may not be related to their gender dysphoria. In an initial assessment, a child psychologist can start to offer developmentally appropriate care for your child.

Therapists, psychologists, and licensed clinical social workers can all provide mental health support for you and your child. But these providers will likely have had varying degrees of experience with LGBTQ+ patients, so don't be shy about asking questions up front to make sure this is a person you and your child will feel safe with. Some religiously affiliated counselors can be wonderful resources, but be sure to talk with them about their views on gender and sexuality to ensure that they will be open to and affirming of your child's gender and sexual exploration and understand that gender diversity is a normal and natural part of the human experience. If this is not how they view gender diversity, they will not be a safe and supportive resource for your child or your family.

Many large hospital systems have or are creating gender-care programs that offer a full menu of services, including endocrinology, gynecology/urology, psychological testing, and support groups for parents, children, and youth. Dr. Wendy Gaultney is a child psychologist who worked at the Kidz Pride Clinic at Metro Health Medical Center in Cleveland, Ohio, with a coordinated team of providers who care for kids and youth experiencing gender dysphoria. At this clinic, which specializes in gender-affirming care, a mental-health assessment is always the first step to determining the best course of care for any patient. Dr. Gaultney says that when young people were experiencing gender dysphoria as well as other mental health issues, the clinicians' approach would be to ask questions about a child's diet, sleep, school environment, and social connections: "Gender-non-conforming kids are just kids, and we treat them as children first and gender-non-conforming kids second."

Another resource that therapists can provide is language that can help a child communicate how they are feeling and help parents understand how they can be supportive. Just introducing ideas and terms like "transgender," "non-binary," "gender fluid," and talking about the differences between expression and identity, can help ease feelings of anxiety or distress and give families a common language to work with. Some parents worry that the introduction of these terms may influence their child in some way; but if children are transgender, they are already wrestling with feelings for which they may not have the language to communicate. The goal of a gender-affirming therapist is to help your child's awareness and articulation of their feelings and sense of identity, even as it shifts and changes.

There are many cultural and societal stigmas that can be barriers to seeking mental health support, but please keep in mind that seeing a therapist is never something to be ashamed of. It's not a sign of weakness but a key part of building your family's community of support. A mental-health diagnosis does not mean there's anything wrong with your child. As it says in the WPATH Standards of Care: "A disorder is a description of something with which a person might struggle, not a description of the person or the person's identity."[16] A diagnosis of

---

[16] "Standards of Care for the Health of Transsexual, Transgender, and Gender Nonconforming People," World Professional Association for Transgender Health Standards of Care, eighth version.

gender dysphoria simply means that a person's expression and understanding of their own gender diversity or transgender identity meets certain medical criteria in order to qualify as a diagnosis, which then enables you to access additional medical services and support for your child's well-being.

To summarize and be clear, a psychologist's diagnosis of gender dysphoria will open up additional, optional medical resources for your child and can enable you to seek coverage of costs from private insurance or Medicaid. Many private insurance companies will cover at least a portion of mental health services (after you meet an annual deductible), and some therapists will offer a sliding scale, so please do not let financial concerns alone prevent you from seeking a therapist if you feel you need this support for you, your child, and/or your family.

⸺

There is a lot of misinformation that is currently being promoted by anti-transgender groups concerning children having surgery or other irreversible medical interventions. In what is clearly a concerted ideological campaign to discourage youth and their parents from seeking gender-affirming care, some political leaders and anti-transgender advocacy groups rely on misinformation and are working to pass restrictive laws in the name of "protecting children." But the science about gender diversity, based on four decades of practice, treatment, and care of transgender and gender non-conforming people of all ages, confirms that gender-affirming care overwhelmingly results in the best health outcomes for transgender children and youth and those who love them.

Please do not worry that taking steps towards gender affirmation means you are making medical decisions immediately. Starting with your child's pediatrician, having conversations with medical professionals about your child's needs based on their stage of development is really essential. If your child has gone through or is in the midst of puberty, your pediatrician will likely refer you to specialists, including endocrinologists who can advise you about medical interventions as well as mental-health support. Gender-affirming medical and mental health providers can help you and your child understand what the different options are at whatever stage of physical and emotional development your child is in. Then together you can make the best decisions with and for your child.

Sometimes when a young person comes out as transgender around the age of puberty, there is a desire on the part of the youth to move quickly to medical treatment. This is often because your child has probably been thinking about this for a long time (even if it is a total surprise to you as parents).

Paula Neira is the Program Director of LGBTQ+ Equity and Education at Johns Hopkins Medicine Office of Diversity, Inclusion, and Health Equity. She is a nurse and social worker (as well as a lawyer and retired Navy officer and also a transgender woman). She first told her mother that she was transgender when she was eleven years old, but in 1974 there wasn't as much support for transgender kids and youth as there is today. Ms. Neira acknowledges that it's normal to feel like you want to rush to change when you know who you are and your body doesn't fit that identity. "But knowing who you are and accepting who you are doesn't always happen at the same time," she says.

When it comes to the medical treatment of adolescents, "Standards of Care for the Health of Transsexual, Transgender, and Gender Nonconforming People" states that "physical interventions should be addressed in the context of adolescent development." Physical interventions for adolescents fall into three categories or stages:

1. *Fully reversible interventions.* These involve the use of hormone suppressing medications ("puberty blockers") which suppress estrogen or testosterone production and consequently delay the physical changes of puberty. Alternative treatment options for adolescents in whom puberty has already advanced include medications that decrease the effects of androgens secreted by the testicles and/ or oral contraceptives to suppress menstruation.

2. *Partially reversible interventions.* These include hormone therapy to masculinize or feminize the body. Some of these hormone-induced changes may need reconstructive surgery to reverse their effect, while other changes are not reversible. Hormone therapy can be started between the ages

of 14-18, depending on a medical professional's recommendation, how long a young person has been living in their affirmed gender identity, and local statues regarding parental consent and other restrictions.

3. *Irreversible interventions.* These are surgical procedures including "top surgery" (chest reconstruction for trans men; breast augmentation for trans women) or genital surgery. According to the WPATH Standards of Care, "Genital surgery should not be carried out until a transgender [youth] has reached the legal age of majority and has lived continuously for at least twelve months in the gender role that is congruent with their gender identity." In some places, genital reconstruction is still required to change a person's gender marker on their birth certificate. However, none of these medical interventions are required for a person to self-identify as transgender or non-binary.

A staged process of medical treatment is recommended to keep options open through the first two stages of transition. The Standards of Care recommend taking adequate time for adolescents and their parents to assimilate fully the effects of earlier interventions before moving to the next stage of medical transition.

Whether or not, or to what extent, these medical interventions are covered by your health insurance can vary. As of 2016 and at least through the writing of this book, however, it is no longer legal for a private insurance company to refuse coverage for gender-affirming care simply because the patient is transgender. Remember, all these decisions about medical interventions to facilitate physical transitions are personal and private decisions, and it's important to have good resources and support of providers you trust in making these choices with and for your child.

~

At some point during your child's gender journey, you and/or your child may find being part of a support group to be helpful. If your child is being treated through a medical system that has an established gender clinic, they will likely offer support groups for both caregivers and patients. Parents and Friends of Lesbians and Gays (PFLAG) is another great place for parents to start, as there are chapters everywhere and many of them offer support groups for parents of trans and gender-diverse people. Within these groups are people with a range of experiences, and the wisdom of other parents and family members can help you feel less alone. Your child may also benefit from meeting other trans or gender-diverse kids or youth. Sometimes these groups are found online, connected with a clinic or mental health provider, or affiliated with a PFLAG chapter. Support groups do not necessarily need to be therapeutic. Just having a safe space to be with other transgender youth can be a valuable source of support.

Max, as I'll call them, is a non-binary high school student who started an online meet-up group for trans elementary/tween-age kids during the Covid-19 pandemic. Max had been working at an aftercare program and really loved spending time with younger kids. But when the pandemic began and schools moved instruction online, Max was worried about the impact that isolation would have, especially on kids who were exploring their gender identity. They reached out through a private Facebook group and found some families who were interested in participating in an online meet-up for gender-diverse teens and tweens. "I thought that what I would have wanted at their age would have been to see people like me as they might be when I got older and to have a chance to meet other trans kids and not feel so alone." Together with another trans girl I'll call Jasmine, they started two groups that met monthly—one for kindergarten through third grade and one fourth-fifth-grade group. At the peak of the pandemic, they had eighteen kids participating in their program, about 3-4 kids each week. Max and Jasmine didn't direct the kids to talk about being transgender, although the kids did bring it up sometimes, but these teen facilitators tried to follow the participants' lead. "I used to be part of a support group that was run by adults, and it was just so depressing because all we talked about was how hard it was to be trans," says Jasmine. Instead, Max and

Jasmine talked with the kids about their favorite animals and transgender celebrities they admire. They invited the kids to draw pictures of themselves when they grow up.

The group disbanded when Max and Jasmine graduated and went off to college but, during such a challenging time, this group was a lifeline for a community of gender-diverse kids and youth to find support and community

~

Gender-affirming care is more than just hormones and surgery; it includes care for the whole person—mind, body, spirit—and often support for the nuclear and extended family. While decisions about medical interventions and addressing mental health issues can be some of the more challenging aspects of having a gender-diverse child, all the ways we care for and support our children are important factors in their well-being, no matter what others may say or think.

More than anything, we parents of transgender and gender-diverse children have to remember that every child is unique. There is no one right path to navigate these decisions, but when we follow our hearts, listen to our kids, and seek out knowledgeable and supportive people to help us along the way, the decisions become much clearer.

QUESTIONS FOR REFLECTION AND DISCUSSION

1. How much do you care about what other people think about how you raise your kids? Explain your answer. Should you care any more or any less about what they think about how you deal with your child's emotional and mental health? Why?

2. Are you hesitant about seeking medical help in general? Explore where that hesitancy comes from. Do you think going to counseling is a kind of admission of failure? Why? How will you work through your own feelings about this in order to meet your child's needs right now?

3. Why do you think that so much political division revolves around sex and gender issues? What are some ways you can bring more understanding and empathy to these conversations?

DATING AND
SEXUALITY

Dating has taught me what I want and don't want,
who I am, and who I want to be.

Jennifer Love Hewitt

actress

When our kids start exploring romantic and sexual relationships, it can be a very trying time for us as parents. We know that this phase of life and their social development is going to come, but we never feel ready for it when it does. And even though we want our kids to experience the joys of a healthy, loving relationship, we can't help but worry about their hearts getting broken. This is even more true when it comes to gender-diverse kids, whose experience of their gender and sexuality is expansive and doesn't fit into the nice, neat boxes our society creates for romantic relationships. Just like all adolescents, transgender youth also need to be able to find healthy models for their dating and sexual lives, which can be challenging in our heteronormative culture. We still have a way to go to destigmatize LGBTQ+ sexuality and relationships in our society.

For gender-diverse kids in particular, online spaces can be liberating and empowering, because they can interact with their peers without disclosing their gender identity if they don't feel comfortable doing so. At the same time, many of them are using social media to "come out" to peers, friends, and family, which can have both positive and negative implications.

Of course, as with any young people, age-appropriate privacy concerns and online safety is essential. As they say, "the Internet is forever" and adolescents need to be made aware of who can view their social media profiles and for how long into the future. In addition, cyber-bullying among young people is still very prevalent. So, knowing who our children are interacting with and what is being shared online is part of our guiding and protecting them. This is obviously and especially true as they are exploring their gender identity.

~

Becoming aware of one's sexual identity is another normal and healthy part of adolescent development. It is important to remember that gender identity is separate and distinct from sexual and romantic attraction and, like their cisgender friends, transgender and gender-diverse youth can be attracted to people of the same, opposite, or non-binary gender identity.

Having open and honest conversations with your kids about intimacy, contraception, sexual consent, and dating is incredibly important to transgender children. For some transgender kids, sexual attraction and intimacy can bring up fears and anxiety, worries about rejection from potential partners, or the triggering of body shame or gender dysphoria. Depending on our experiences, we parents may be working through our own complicated relationships with sex and our bodies. That's why it's so important for us to do our own mental and emotional work to embrace a healthy relationship with our own bodies and sexuality so that we can help our kids to feel confident and safe and to know their bodies are wonderful and beautiful and worthy of love.

On our second date way back in 1999, my husband Marcus and I went to see the movie *Boys Don't Cry* staring Hillary Swank as Brandon Teena. The film, for which Swank won a best-actress Academy Award, is based on the real-life story of a young transgender man living in a small town in Nebraska. As with much of the media portrayals of transgender people, this film focused on how much time and energy trans people spend hiding their true self. In the beginning of the film, for example, Brandon has to run away from home because his ex-girlfriend's brother discovers that Brandon is transgender and threatens his life. Later in the film, Brandon falls in love with a woman, but when her friends find out Brandon's secret, they brutally assault him.

This film's release was a year after Matthew Shephard was killed by two men in Wyoming for being gay. The defense attorney for Shephard's murderer used a "panic defense," explaining that Matthew was killed because he made a sexual advance towards a boy named Aaron McKinney that angered McKinney so much that he killed Matthew. Both Aaron McKinney and his accomplice, Russell Henderson, were convicted and are serving life sentences; but the anti-gay and anti-trans "panic defense" is still legal in most states and attempts to ban it at a federal level in recent years have failed.

⌒

Naturally, when our son Evan came out as transgender, stories such as these were part of Marcus' and my limited awareness of the lives of LGBTQ+ people. But today we know many trans and non-binary people who are proud of who they are, are comfortable in their own identity and sexuality, and have found healthy loving relationships. There is also significantly more positive representation of queer love and relationships in our popular culture for kids to see their own experiences reflected. It's true that transgender people can have some unique experiences to navigate when it comes to dating and romantic partnerships, but their gender identity need not prevent them from succeeding in what is, after all, among the most natural of human instincts. Two of the most attractive qualities in human beings are first knowing who they are and then being confident in who they are, regardless of their gender or sexual orientation. Our job as parents is simply to help our children develop those two qualities.

One of the unique experiences for transgender and gender-fluid youth who are starting to explore romantic relationships is deciding when and how to disclose their gender identity to a potential partner. Because being cisgender is the default assumption in our culture, this can, therefore, be a fraught decision. Our kids may choose to share this information up front with all potential partners, so that they can be sure that any person they might become romantically involved with accepts them for who they are. Or perhaps they will wait until after they have gotten to know each other and hope the partner will not care (or has already assumed or guessed) that they are transgender. Or, if they fear the relationship might not develop, they don't want to have "outed" themselves unnecessarily.

There is no right answer to these questions—every person and every relationship is unique. And as children get to the age that they are dating and becoming sexually active, parents cannot make these decisions for them. Our role is simply to engage in conversation with our child at the earliest age appropriate and encourage and enable them to develop the relational skills to navigate their sexual attractions and romances themselves, always making clear that they can share their feelings and questions with us as they are ready. This may also require us, as parents, to work through our own feelings, worries, and hopes with our partner, trusted friends, or a therapist so we can be supportive of our child without overreacting.

With any child, regardless of gender identity or sexual orientation, we need to make sure that they have good, accurate information about contraception and safe sexual practices. A gender-affirming pediatrician can help us make sure that our kids are fully informed. Most doctors recommend vaccination against HPV for all adolescents around the age of 11-13, and we parents should still encourage our kids to use condoms to prevent STIs if they become sexually active. A couple of sex-positive books for youth that are inclusive of LGBTQ+ youth are

Sex is a Funny Word and *You Know, Sex*—both by Cory Silverberg and Fiona Smyth.

We want our children to develop healthy sexuality and relationships with their own bodies as well as consensual relationships with their partners. In Elijah Nealy's book *Transgender Children and Youth: Cultivating Pride and Joy with Families in Transition*, he notes that transgender youth are often asked intrusive and inappropriate questions about their bodies and sexuality, often by people who have no right to ask these types of questions. But as parents, we can help our kids think through their sexual identities alongside their gender identities in order to develop healthy attitudes about their own sexual identity and sexuality. Dr. Nealy suggests some questions we might want to invite our kids to consider:

- What are your feelings about the parts of your body that are often associated with sexuality?
- Do your feelings about these parts of your body interfere with your ability to be intimate with a partner?
- How do your gender and biological sex impact the kinds of sexual activities in which you engage (or won't engage), either on your own or with others?

Whether our children are transgender or cisgender, isn't our hope that they will make responsible, healthy choices; choose romantic partners who will love and respect them; and find love that helps them flourish throughout their life? The dating world has radically changed with the advent of online dating, and there are things that our transgender kids will have to navigate about dating we may never have experienced personally. But we can still provide support and guidance, keeping lines of communication open so that our kids will be able to engage in healthy, loving, romantic relationships.

QUESTIONS FOR REFLECTION AND DISCUSSION FOR PARENTS

1. Recall your own sex-education. Were your parents helpful...or not? How do you want to be with your own child or children? How will you prepare yourself to be so?
2. How upfront do you think children should be with people they are dating about gender issues? Why? Now, what does your child think? Listen carefully. If the two of you need help sorting this out, seek professional advice.
3. Do you think being cisgender will or should always be the fallback assumption in society? Give your reasons. Now imagine a world where there are no assumptions about people's sexual or gender orientation. How might that work?

SPEAKING UP/ SPEAKING OUT

It took me quite a long time to develop a voice,
and now that I have it,
I am not going to be silent.

Madeleine Albright
former Secretary of State of the
United States of America

Even as you yourself are learning more about gender identities, transgender issues, and how to best support your gender-diverse child, your family and friends—maybe even strangers—will start to approach you for information on the subject. They may even expect you to be an expert and have answers to all their questions.

This can feel overwhelming, believe me, because I have been there, and the pressure to act like an "expert" was part of what moved me to want to write this book. But of course I am not an expert—I continue learning new things from this experience, and so will you. Although there are increasingly more helpful and credible resources available where you can turn for information, you will likely find yourself needing to provide guidance and answer questions for others, even as you are still figuring things out yourself.

~

When Charlotte's daughter Aria, as I call her, transitioned at age seven, one of the places where her family turned for support was their faith community. The church had already been explicit about their welcoming of lesbian and gay people for some time; and so, as Charlotte's extended family expected, the church was very supportive of Aria. But because she was the first trans person to come out in their church, the leadership didn't really have a lot of information or resources to offer.

"Just tell us what we should do," the pastor said to Charlotte. And while this is a much better response than she might have received from many faith communities, this type of well-meaning response still placed the responsibility back on Charlotte to bring the church along in order to help the congregation know how to support the little girl. Especially when this issue is all new to us, and when our kids are still figuring out who they are, and when we are learning how to support them, adding the additional burden of educating others can be a daunting responsibility for us parents as we navigate this daring adventure.

The first conversation we need to have is the one with our kids and our partners about how public to be about our family's experience. There are always risks involved in sharing your story, and as parents this gender journey is only partly our story to tell. We must respect our children's privacy and how they feel about being "out" to the wider world at various stages of their life.

The second thing we need to always keep in mind is that we cannot speak for all transgender or gender-diverse kids or their families. Especially if you, like me, are heterosexual and cisgender, we are not coming into this with much personal knowledge or experience. We are definitely *not* experts. Sure, we can and will share what we have learned along the way from our personal history, but every child and family's experience is unique, so we need not and should not try and speak for all families or situations.

As the parent of a transgender or gender-diverse kid, you may, at times, find yourself in the role of educator, advocate, and probably a whole lot of other things you didn't think you had signed up for. Some parents relish this role, like Katie, a parent of a transgender girl in North Carolina who decided to go to law school at the age of forty-five because she believed that would be the best way to advocate for her daughter, Maddie. "Maddie will probably need legal support throughout her life unless things drastically change in this country," Katie told *The Washington Post.* "She's going to need somebody to fight for her on those legal fronts, and who better to fight for her than her own mom?"[17]

Katie's commitment is truly inspirational, but it's probably not an option for most of us to quit our jobs and go to law school to fight for our kids' rights. Nor is it necessary. All of us have our own gifts, passions, and spheres of influence where we can make a difference in creating a world that is safe and affirming of transgender youth. The key is to focus our energy on what each child needs most right now and where you believe you can make the biggest difference for your own and other kids like them.

You cannot fight on all fronts at once, you know that. So, where are the places, and who are the people, where

[17] "Her child is transgender. So she went back to school and became a lawyer to help fight for trans rights," Sydney Page, *Washington Post,* July 26, 2021

your child most needs you to lean in and speak up? Their school? Your faith community? Your nuclear or extended family? Most importantly, focus on creating one safe and affirming space at a time for your child. When our kids see us as allies of transgender people out in the world, they will know that they have our full support at home, too.

Of course, you can start just by making sure your home is the most safe, the most welcoming, and the most affirming place it can possibly be for your kids and their friends. Then, if you've got time and energy left, you can help other parents learn and understand that if they have children who are gender diverse or gender fluid it is *their* most important job to help *them*.

~

As a parent of a transgender or gender-diverse child, you do have a voice and an important experience to share, when you are ready. Together, by speaking out, we parents can help normalize the experience of gender diversity as just another aspect of what it means to parent in today's environment. By sharing what we have learned, how we have struggled and coped, what resources are available, and how we have learned and grown, we can help foster greater understanding, compassion, and awareness about trans and non-binary identity and create safer spaces for our children and children like ours to thrive.

With so much political focus on transgender issues right now, there is a growing opportunity for us to share our stories more publicly, which will help counter misinformation and fearmongering. A few years ago, a young transgender girl in New Jersey, Rebekah Bruesehoff, went to a rally after the federal government rolled back protections for transgender students. Her mom took a picture of Rebekah holding a hand-made sign that read, "I'm the scary transgender person the media warned you about," and the photo went viral on social media.[18] Rebekah, now a national activist, has been featured on Disney's Marvel Heroes Project, has testified before the New Jersey legislature, and is part of the Gender Cool Project, which works to "replace misinformed opinions with positive experiences of meeting transgender and non-binary youth who are thriving."[19]

By writing letters to the editor of your local paper, sharing your family's story on social media, or just talking with trusted friends, family, and neighbors about your experience of having a gender-diverse child, you can be part of changing some people's hearts and minds. When she was ready to be more public about her family's journey, Jennifer Roth-Burnette wrote a beautifully honest and thoughtful piece about her child's coming out experience on the online public forum *Medium*. While she and her husband had been open from the beginning with family, friends, and their church about having a transgender child, publishing this essay shared their experience as a family with a much broader audience.

---

[18] https://www.rebekahbruesehoff.com
[19] https://gendercool.org

Among the many supportive comments that Jennifer's piece received was one from someone named Denise who wrote, "Beautiful story. I appreciate how honest you are about the conversations and your willingness to critique how you navigate this. I've never been in your shoes so I can only imagine how hard it is to simultaneously convey love and acceptance and provide the guidance a child needs." Jennifer's willingness to share her own parenting journey in such a public way helped others see the experience of a transgender teen from the perspective of a mother seeking to support her child through a difficult transition.

A further step beyond storytelling is moving into advocacy or organizing on behalf of transgender people and their rights. It has been said about many issues that "the personal is political" and this is certainly true right now about the rights of transgender and gender-fluid kids. As this book goes to print, there is an unprecedented attack on transgender youth in which some state legislatures are seeking to limit their access to healthcare, their ability to participate in sports, or the teaching about LGBTQ+ history in schools. The National Center for Transgender Equality (NCTE) tracks anti-transgender legislation across the country and offers resources on knowing your legal rights and various issues from healthcare to housing to employment, where transgender people often face discrimination.

NCTE also worked together with other leading LGBTQ+ advocacy groups to create a guide for parents titled *Going Public: Is Public Advocacy Right for You and Your Family?* This helpful guide encourages parents who are interested in public action to find a network of support with other parents and activists, to prioritize their own self-care and family boundaries, and to take important security steps before engaging in public advocacy.[20]

As parents, our voices matter a great deal and can have a huge impact. You don't have to have a large platform or focus on national or even state legislation to be involved in activism. You might be able to work with other parents through your PTA to advocate for more gender-inclusive school curriculum, establish a Gender and Sexuality Alliance, or help develop policies that protect transgender and non-binary students in your school. You might organize an educational event at your place of worship to introduce people to transgender issues and make your community a more welcoming place. You might choose to focus on a sport your child plays and make sure the league is welcoming and inclusive of transgender and non-binary youth.

There are lots of other ways to engage in the work of educating and advocating for our kids; but not all parents feel comfortable in this role, and that's okay, too. However and whenever you might choose to use your voice and your influence on behalf of your child, it will help grow

[20] https://transequality.org/sites/default/files/docs/resources/A%20Guide%20for%20Parents%20of%20Transgender%20and%20Gender-Expansive%20Youth%201-10-18.pdf

the movement to ensure that the world is safer and more accepting for all transgender and non-binary people.

⁓

Because the experience of fighting for your child's needs can feel overwhelming sometimes and just caring for your family may be all you feel equipped to manage, when other people come to you with their questions or looking for more information about the transgender experience, it's also perfectly acceptable for you to set boundaries. You can simply direct others to good places you know they can find information with which to educate themselves.

No one should ever expect you to be an expert on LGBTQ+ issues just because one or more of your children are trans, or to become a public spokesperson for transgender or gender-diversity issues. And you shouldn't place that responsibility on yourself, either. But the more we parents learn and live through our own child's experience, we do have an important perspective to offer, even if it's just to other parents whose kids are also exploring their gender identity. Being part of a community where many people are sharing stories and experiences and working together for change can feel empowering and hopeful, and I encourage you to find ways of participating in this great community as you are ready to do so.

QUESTIONS FOR REFLECTION AND DISCUSSION

1. Have you ever spoken out or been involved in any non-gender-related controversial public issues? If so, tell how you felt in that process. Are you more or less inclined to get involved in issues that affect your children? Explain why.

2. Write a simple "boundaries statement" with and for your nuclear or extended family on when, why, to whom, and how you will share information on your child's or children's situation regarding gender identity. Revisit the statement at least once a year and update it as necessary.

3. What are the elements of a "safe, affirming space" for your child? Is your home one now? If not, how do you make it so? If it is, how can you help find/make another one for your children outside the home?

AFTERWORD

The best way out is always through.

Robert Frost

Your child is still, mostly, a kid; and you are, and always will be, your child's parent, no matter how old they (or you) become. Having a trans or gender-diverse kid affects some things, but it doesn't change the basic truth: Your child needs to be loved, encouraged, supported, taught, disciplined, and guided by you to adulthood.

It's as simple, and as complex, as simply loving and supporting your child through all the ups and downs of their life, including their gender identity. Support looks like lots of different things, depending on your child and the stage of life and of this gender journey where you now find yourselves. Sometimes support means navigating health-care systems, advocating for or with your child at school, or taking them shopping for new clothes to help them express themselves more fully. Support can also simply look like stepping back and allowing them the space to figure things out and providing that space of safety and love when they need you.

And I promise you, there will come a time when your child's gender identity is not all you or they think about. In time, it will become just one more beautiful part of who they are as a human being, integrated into the richness of your lives.

Friends, welcome to this daring adventure. Buckle up and settle in. You've got this!

SOME HELPFUL TERMS

(in alphabetical order)

Cisgender: A person whose gender identity aligns with their biological sex or the gender assigned to them at birth.

Gender diversity: Gender diversity is an umbrella term that is used to describe gender identities that demonstrate a diversity of expression beyond the binary framework. For many gender-diverse people, the concept of binary gender—having to choose to express yourself as male or female—is limiting and unnatural.

Gender (or body) dysphoria: Broadly defined as discomfort or distress that is caused by a discrepancy between a person's gender identity and that person's sex assigned at birth and the associated gender role and/or primary and secondary sex characteristics. (See WPATH Standards of Care, eighth version.)

Gender expression: The way in which a person expresses their gender identity through choice of clothing, hair, etc.

This gender expression is also on a spectrum and does not necessarily correspond with cultural norms of gender identity.

Gender fluidity: Gender-fluid people are people whose gender changes over time. They might also identify as a-gender, bi-gender, or another nonbinary identity.

Gender identity: One's innermost concept of self as male, female, a blend of both or neither. It is how individuals perceive themselves and what they call themselves. One's gender identity can be the same or different from the sex assigned at birth.

Gender neutral: An additional term used by and for people who do not identify with the gender binary. People who are gender neutral choose not to label their gender, identifying more as a person or human being than any gender at all.

Gender non-conforming: Denoting or relating to a person whose behavior or appearance does not conform to prevailing cultural and social expectations about what is appropriate to their gender.

LGBTQ+: A common acronym that stands for Lesbian, Gay, Bisexual, Transgender, Queer/Questioning. Sometimes the letters "I" (for Intersex) and "A" (for Asexual) are also added, or a plus sign is used to include the many identities that are part of the diverse gender and sexuality community. Among some Indigenous communities, "2S" (for "Two Spirit") is used. Some people use the term *queer* to reclaim this slur that has been used against LGBTQ+ persons. *Queer* also encompasses many different intersections of gender, gender expression, and sexuality that are present within the community.

Non-binary: The socially constructed idea that there are only two genders is called "gender binary," because binary means "having two parts" (male and female). Therefore, "non-binary" is one term people use to describe a gender identity that doesn't fall into one of these two categories, male or female, but is something more, different, or unique that does not conform to the "gender-binary" designation.

Transgender: A broad term, denoting or relating to a person whose sense of personal identity and gender does not correspond with the sex assigned to them at birth. While a person's physical anatomy generally corresponds to their biological sex, it does not necessarily determine their gender identity.

RECOMMENDATIONS FOR FURTHER READING

For Parents/Caregivers:

Transgender Children and Youth: Cultivating Pride and Joy with Families in Transition, Elijah C Nealy, 2017, W.W. Norton and Co. Inc.

The Transgender Teen: A Handbook for Parents and Professionals Supporting Transgender and Non-Binary Teens, Stephanie Brill and Lisa Kenney, 2016, Cleis Press

For Kids and Youth:

The Gender Book, by Mel Reiff Hill and Jay Mays, 2013, Marshall House Press

The Gender Identity Workbook for Kids: A Guide to Exploring Who You Are, Kelly Storck, 2018, Instant Help Books

Queerfully and Wonderfully Made: A Guide for LGBTQ+ Christian Teens, Leigh Finke, editor, 2020, Beaming Books

For Leaders and Members of Faith Communities:

A Brief Guide to Ministry with LGBTQIA Youth, Cody J. Sanders, 2017, Westminster John Knox Press

Transforming: The Bible and the Lives of Transgender Christians, Austen Hartke, 2018, Westminster John Knox Press

Trans-gender: Theology, Ministry, and Communities of Faith (Second Edition), Justin Sabia-Tanis, 2018, Wipf & Stock Publishers

SUGGESTIONS FOR FAITH COMMUNITIES

In all you do, strive to create a safe, affirming space for young people of all backgrounds. Pay attention to it. Celebrate it. Fund it. Make it accessible to all young people, even if they are not members of your congregation. Here are ten specific suggestions how you might do that.

1. Make sure your sermons, liturgy and religious education curricula are sensitive to the issues of sexuality and gender identity and are positively representative of LGBTQIA+ persons and experiences.
2. Consider what liturgies or celebrations you already have to mark transitions in people's lives. How might you begin to design rituals for young people who are coming out or transitioning in their sexual and gender identities?
3. Develop a small lending library of books and other resources that deal positively on the issues of gender and sexual identity. Organize the books and

videos into age-appropriate sections and advertise the availability of the material to the entire community. Sponsor book clubs on books written by people of different gender identities.

4. Bring in guest speakers or preachers who are transgender and invite them to share their story or talk about another subject in which they have knowledge and expertise.

5. Organize a clothing drive or clothing closet where the youth in your community who are exploring their gender identity can try on clothes to help them express who are coming to know themselves to be.

6. Research the summer camps in your community to determine which are safe and affirming for LGBTQIA+ youth. Perhaps start a scholarship fund to send youth from your faith community to one or more of them.

7. Work with members of your local school board to advocate for the needs of transgender and gender-diverse students within the school system.

8. Learn what kinds of resources are available in your community to support gender diverse youth. For example, are there support groups in your community for gender-diverse youth and their caregivers? Who are the gender-affirming therapists and medical professionals in your area? Do they take most insurance, Medicaid, or offer a sliding scale payment structure?

9. Educate yourself on the laws in your state regarding gender-affirming care for children and youth. If gender-affirming care is not protected or is banned in your state, seek out advocacy groups that are working to challenge those laws. Write letters or op-eds—either as individuals or as a faith community—to your lawmakers or local newspapers about the importance of gender-affirming care.

10. Adopt or develop a program for sexual education for all teens and young adults in your faith community that is welcoming to all and inclusive of those who are LGBTQIA+.

ACKNOWLEDGEMENTS

This book has been a labor of love, and I am grateful for the many people who helped me bring it into the world.

First and foremost, I want to offer my deepest thanks to all those who were willing to be interviewed for this book: the Pinwheel families and many other parents of transgender kids, as well as the kids and youth themselves, who were willing to speak with me so openly and honestly about their experiences. You all inspire me with your love, courage, and wisdom!

Thank you to Paula Neira, Program Director of LGBTQ+ Equity and Education at Johns Hopkins Medicine Office of Diversity, Inclusion, and Health Equity, and to Dr. Wendy Galutney. Both of their knowledge and experience with the medical and mental health resources for transgender kids has been invaluable.

Thank you to those trusted friends who read the many versions of this book along the way: Kara Scroggins, Amy McCullough, Laura Elkins, and Karla Kramer.

Thank you to the endlessly creative Wendy Hudgins for her help with the cover design and to Andrea Reider for her interior design and typesetting.

Thank you to my editor, Greg Piece, for providing so much helpful guidance to this first-time author.

Thank you to the faith community of Dumbarton United Methodist Church in Washington, DC, for allowing me the time to write this book and for being a leader for more than thirty-five years for full inclusion of LGBTQIA+ persons in the life of the church. And thanks to all the queer folks there who have taught me so much about what it means to be a faithful Christian.

And most of all, thank you to my family, friends and colleagues who gave their support and encouragement all along the way. For everyone who asked, "How is your book coming?" or said, "I can't wait to read it," well, here it is at last!

ABOUT THE AUTHOR

R ev. Rachel Cornwell (she/her) is a United Methodist pastor in Washington, DC, and the parent of three amazing kids, the youngest of whom first came out as transgender when he was in first grade. This is Rachel's first book. It was inspired by her journey as both a parent and a pastor and written to offer specific support to other parents of gender-diverse kids and their faith communities in fostering more affirming families and safer communities for transgender kids and youth.

The author with her family (2019)

ADVANCE PRAISE FOR *DARING ADVENTURES*

Every human being should read Rev. Rachel Cornwell's *Daring Adventures: Helping Gender-Diverse Kids and Their Families Thrive*. I am an out transgender person for thirty-five years and a parent of a non-binary teen. I wish I could have referred this book to my clients over the years. It gives parents the skills they need to show up for their children while still engaging powerfully in their own faith communities.
—Jay Pryor, queer speaker, author, company CEO

Offers compassionate guidance to parents of trans young people and also younger children just beginning to explore their gender identity. Especially valuable to readers rooted in a faith tradition. Weaving her own heartfelt story into accounts from other parents, Rachel Cornwell provides a hopeful path for all people of good will seeking to understand and support gender-diverse children. —Katherine Reynolds Lewis, journalist, author of *The Good News about Bad Behavior: Why Kids Are Less Disciplined Than Ever—And What to Do About It*

My mom struggled with my transition at first, but as time passed she said, "If I had only known when you were a kid, maybe I could have done something to help you." Today, parents' help is both welcome and possible. *Daring Adventures* is like a care package, assembled with a mother's love and packed especially for those folks lucky enough to be parenting a trans child. —Rev. Junia Joplin, pastor, Metropolitan Community Church of Toronto

Daring Adventures **is the beautiful book** that all of our beautiful families need. From a relentlessly child-centered place, Rev. Cornwell has created connection for the many of us who are journeying with gender-fluid children and seeking to understand, advocate, and parent well. She gives parents the sense that we are not alone. —Rev. Dr. Jennifer Harvey, author of *Raising White Kids: Bringing Up Children in a Racially Unjust America*